THE PSYCHOLOGY
OF WELLBEING

How can we improve our sense of wellbeing? What explains the current wellbeing boom? What does wellbeing mean to you?

The Psychology of Wellbeing offers readers tools to navigate their own wellbeing and understand what makes a 'good life'. Using self-reflection and storytelling, it explores how trust affects psychological and emotional wellbeing, considers how stress and inequality impact our psychological wellbeing, and how trends such as positive psychology influence our understanding of happiness.

In a world where the 'wellness economy' is big business, The Psychology of Wellbeing shows how we can question and make sense of information sources and sheds light on the wellness, self-care, and self-help industry.

Gary W. Wood is a chartered psychologist, solution-focused life coach, and broadcaster. He is widely quoted in the media for expert analysis, for coaching tips, and as a featured advice columnist (agony uncle). He is a fellow of the Higher Education Academy and has taught psychology, research methods, and learning skills in several UK universities. He also consults on social policy research for government bodies, broadcasting regulators, health organizations, and charities. Gary has published in academic journals on psychology and health and is the author of self-help books. These include Don't Wait for Your Ship to Come In, Swim Out to Meet It, which has been translated into several languages, and Unlock Your Confidence. He also wrote The Psychology of Gender for the first wave of the Psychology of Everything series, and Letters to a New Student. Gary is in private practice as a life and wellbeing coach, trainer, and research consultant. He is based in Birmingham and Edinburgh, UK. See: www.drgarywood.co.uk

THE PSYCHOLOGY OF EVERYTHING

People are fascinated by psychology, and what makes humans tick. Why do we think and behave the way we do? We've all met armchair psychologists claiming to have the answers, and people that ask if psychologists can tell what they're thinking. The Psychology of Everything is a series of books which debunk the popular myths and pseudo-science surrounding some of life's biggest questions.

The series explores the hidden psychological factors that drive us, from our subconscious desires and aversions, to our natural social instincts. Absorbing, informative, and always intriguing, each book is written by an expert in the field, examining how research-based knowledge compares with popular wisdom, and showing how psychology can truly enrich our understanding of modern life.

Applying a psychological lens to an array of topics and contemporary concerns – from sex, to fashion, to conspiracy theories – The Psychology of Everything will make you look at everything in a new way.

Titles in the series:

For further information about this series please visit
www.routledgetextbooks.com/textbooks/thepsychologyofeverything/

THE
PSYCHOLOGY
OF WELLBEING

GARY W. WOOD

Routledge
Taylor & Francis Group

LONDON AND NEW YORK

First published 2021
by Routledge
2 Park Square, Milton Park, Abingdon, Oxon OX14 4RN

and by Routledge
52 Vanderbilt Avenue, New York, NY 10017

Routledge is an imprint of the Taylor & Francis Group, an informa business

British Library Cataloguing-in-Publication Data
A catalogue record for this book is available from the British Library

Library of Congress Cataloging-in-Publication Data
A catalog record for this book has been requested

ISBN: 978-0-367-89809-0 (hbk)
ISBN: 978-0-367-89808-3 (pbk)
ISBN: 978-1-003-02125-4 (ebk)

Typeset in Joanna
by Apex CoVantage, LLC

Printed and bound by CPI Group (UK) Ltd, Croydon, CR0 4YY

CONTENTS

ACKNOWLEDGEMENTS

Thank you to everyone who supported the writing process and my wellbeing. As always, countless thanks to Dr Takeshi Fujisawa, for practical, technical, and emotional support, as well as for encouragement, patience, and cake and reminding me to back up, back up, back up. I couldn't have finished this book without him.

It is always a joy to work with Eleanor Taylor at Routledge. This book, and earlier ones, benefited hugely from her constructive and insightful feedback. Thanks also to those who reviewed the proposal for the book and offered useful comments on the book's structure and helped me to tell a better story. And thanks to Chris Mathews and the team at Apex CoVantage for typesetting and proof-reading. A big thank you to Trisha Greenhalgh, 'Brown', and Neha Sheokand (at Taylor & Francis) for kindly responding to my requests for copies of material. Thanks also to Jonathan Foster for his swift response to my question about a quotation about journalism sometimes attributed to him. And special thanks, as always, to the Society of Authors for contractual advice and support during my writing career.

I dedicate this book to my grandparents, Nelly Florence Butcher and Clifford Bertram Butcher. It is also dedicated to my dear friend Dr Thomas F. Pagel (1940–2019) from Kalamazoo, Michigan. I'll miss his wry take on things, his encouragement, advice, and generosity of spirit. He had a much higher opinion of me and my abilities than I've ever had myself. It always meant a lot.

PREFACE

Sociologist William Simon writes 'All attempts at theorizing social life are, at the same time, works of autobiography'.[1] I've joked more than once that 'this wellbeing book will be the death of me'.[2] And that wasn't so far from the truth. A major depressive episode during late 2019[3] didn't help the writing process. Neither did another attack of lower-back pain, a tooth broken beyond repair, and finding a lump in my armpit.[4] And all this amidst start of the Novel Coronavirus pandemic. It caused me to question if psychology had anything to say about improving wellbeing. And even if it did, was I fit and ready to write it? Also, this book is part of a bigger story – a series called 'The Psychology of Everything'. And, I realized I've never stopped to ask if psychology does have something to say about everything.[5] And yet, somehow, here we are.

Before starting this book, I thought it was lexicographer, Dr Samuel Johnson who wrote 'a writer only begins a book. A reader finishes it'. But we cannot pinpoint where Johnson wrote it.[6] We just find traces of others telling us he did. But whoever said it, the sentiment holds true. Books are paths crossed in the autobiographies of writers and readers – even if we share just a page, or a few lines.[7] In this book, I tell a story of the psychology of wellbeing. And as you reflect and take the story forward, it's critical for you to know where it came from. Within reason, I've tried to let my voice come through, albeit with fewer expletives and without phrases particular to my regional dialect.[8]

I was the first in my family to go to University. I was a mature student, at least on paper. And it wasn't planned. It happened as a series of unfortunate events that I tried to make sense of. And when faced with life decisions, I chose the path I hadn't trod before. It was often on a 'what-have-you-got-to-lose' basis. I studied Human Psychology in an Applied Psychology department, which has shaped everything I do. At University, I credit one charismatic lecturer as giving me 'permission to think'.[9] And, since then, I've always seen it as part of my job to 'pay it forward'. My doctoral research was in attitudes and stereotypes and the 'intolerance of ambiguity' And, I still think we are more likely to find 'truth' in 'shades of grey'. I got into coaching, after I became, unofficially, the 'go-to' person for students, while teaching psychology. Later I took my first training course in coaching to help boost the confidence and skills of a group of mature, part-time, evening class students. This led to me running extra-curricular personal development courses that, in turn, became the basis for a book.[10]

If you hadn't guessed, by now, politically, I'm left-libertarian.[11] Nominally, I'd be classified a ~~'white male'~~.[12] I've traced my family tree and I'm very, very English - again, at least on paper. But that's not who I am, and it does not overwrite or erase my lived experience or my values.[13] From, the light-hearted gender test in Kate Bornstein's *My Gender Workbook*, I'm a 'gender outlaw'.[14] I'm the 'odd boy' who doesn't like sport[15] and slightly clumsy and a bit body dysmorphic. My longest relationships have been based on shared values rather than shared demographics. As far back as I can remember, unfamiliar cultures have attracted me, perhaps because I have often felt like an outsider in my own. My first memory of calling out prejudice was, around age five, watching Western films. And at the age of 14 years of age I was beaten by a teacher with a bamboo cane across the hand for impertinently challenging *his* racist comments to another boy.

While drafting this book I, retook the *Values in Action Inventory of Character Strengths*. It seemed like a good displacement activity, at the time. It was either that or declutter. My values/strengths came out, in order, as a *love of learning, love, bravery, kindness, humour, curiosity, appreciation of beauty, honesty, creativity,* and *judgement*.[16]

Sociologist Stanislav Andreski contends that 'anybody who searches for the truth about human affairs and then reveals it cannot avoid treading upon some toes.'[17] And, if I've done my job right, it might burst a few bubbles, pull rugs or even cause the odd existential shrug. But hopefully, it will empower too. It isn't a 'because I say so' kind of book. I view writing as an act of rebellion. My approach coaching is the same. I encourage people to be themselves (or transcend themselves) despite themselves.

The best advice I ever had for writing was 'you don't finish a book, you abandon it'[18]. So here it is. Over to you.

1

INTRODUCTION

Defining wellbeing, psychology, and the self

THE WELLBEING BOOM

Questions of how to 'live the good life' and to 'live long and prosper'[1] have occupied us for thousands of years. But it is modern academic research in psychology that has led the current 'wellbeing boom'. More of us now spend more time talking about it, reading about it, researching it, and writing about it. From magazines to self-help books, from workplace reports to government papers, its pull is far-reaching. And, even if we cannot agree on how to spell it, we can, at least, concur that wellbeing[2] is big business. In 2017, globally, the 'wellness economy' was estimated at $42 trillion, and it shows no signs of slowing.[3] That's a lot of wellbeing! Or is it? With so much on offer, it grows ever tougher to sift the science from the 'snake oil'. We are spoilt for choice.

With a glut of wellbeing information, how do we decide what works, what doesn't, and what's just hype? And how do we know what makes a 'good life'? Is it financial security or good relationships? Is it having a purpose in life and setting goals? Is it being mindful or grateful? Is it all down to positive thinking, or simply good luck?[4] Or, is it 'a little bit of everything'? And in our quest to find the answers, in what or whom do we put our trust? Do we rely on scientists, academics, and doctors? Or do we listen to the politicians who tell us that 'people have had enough of experts'?[5] What then? Do we count on journalists, self-help authors, media pundits, self-styled gurus, and bloggers to filter information for us? Or maybe we take our lead from 'Karen' on Facebook,[6] or the 'friend of a friend' who 'knows someone'. And let us not forget our everyday appeals to the authority of the mysterious 'they' who always have lots to say about everything.[7] How do we spot the breakthroughs from the fake news? How do we get the upper hand and make sense of it all?

THE PLAN

The Psychology of Wellbeing is a short, accessible exploration to bridge the gaps between 'everyday' ideas, pop psychology,[8] and academic knowledge. It is chiefly about psychological wellbeing. But it also deals with aspects of physical health that affect cognition, emotions, and moods. It is not possible, in this slim volume, to review all on offer in the 'shopping cart' of wellness. Instead, the book focuses on critical skills and offers a framework to assess questions around wellbeing.[9] To meet these goals, it uses self-reflection and storytelling as learning devices. This strategy helps to shed light on the common ground between self-help books and current approaches to research methods. We just need the tools – something to help structure our reflections and analyze our storytelling.

It is standard, in academic psychology, to clarify the key terms of the debate. These are short, working definitions[10] to align readers, writers, and researchers. But we begin with a personal definition of wellbeing – what it means to you, because reflection is a vital part of the learning process.[11] Your version provides the basis to examine academic meanings. Then, each chapter in the book offers a chance to refine your definitions, both personal and formal. In this way, it also gives *a gentle nod* to the self-help genre.[12]

Our tour begins with familiar, social enquiries about our wellbeing and how we respond.

EVERYDAY WELLBEING

How are you? How are you doing? Are you well?

We ask and answer questions about each other's wellness countless times during our lives. But what goes through your mind during these everyday happenings? Some years ago, I had a comical stay at a bed-and-breakfast guesthouse. On greeting the owner with 'Good morning. How are you today?' he snapped back, 'Do you really care?'[13] I was taken aback, but it's a valid point. In routine exchanges about wellness, how do you tell real interest from polite social ritual? Consider how your questions and replies vary across settings and times and with different people. How do you know when to give the full story, the edited highlights, or something vague but civil? In reacting to this simple question, there is a complex process at play. These interactions show how we tap into pre-existing scripts that we edit 'on the fly' to tell our life stories, as we go.

Now, if a psychologist asked about your wellbeing, how might you answer? Or, if you had to draft an essay or a report on wellbeing, where would you start? And how would your personal definition differ from a general one?

Pause for a moment to reflect, and then read on.

DEFINING THE TERMS OF THE DEBATE

In academic examinations, first we take a moment to read the questions and spot the keywords. Consider the question 'How can psychology help us to understand wellbeing?' The keywords *psychology* and *wellbeing* infer other concepts. Wellbeing implies a sense of the 'being' that is being well — the *Self*. It is a concept central to both evidence-based academic psychology and the self-help genre in pop psychology. And to explain what psychology is, we need to consider what it does, how it's done, and who does it. The earlier question suggests that psychology will be helpful and aid understanding. But helpful to whom? And, whose understanding will it aid? These questions are the basis of our critical analysis. So, let's take a step back and start with a working definition of the self.

What is the self?

Taken-for-granted concepts can be the most difficult to 'pin down'. Surely, the self is self-explanatory. The self is who you are. But saying 'it is what it is' doesn't tell us much. The psychology of the self could fill several volumes, and we only have limited space here. So, before we get to know it, respect it, be true to it, be well in it, help it, or reinvent it, we need to have, at least, an idea of what 'it' is.[14] Let's open with the self as 'your sense of you as a separate, distinctive, experiencing being'.[15] This concept includes the impression that the self is constant and predictable. It also includes a personal evaluation, known as your self-esteem.[16] It helps to think of your self-concept as your centre of gravity.[17] In psychology, it plays a vital part in motivation, cognition, affect, and social identity.[18] Your sense of self extends to all aspects of your life, from the clothes you wear to the choices you make. So, consider as a starting point what distinguishes and separates you from other experiencing beings. All these factors affect your idea of wellbeing. That is, whether you want to attain and maintain it, or read or write about it.

What is wellbeing?

Wellbeing is another concept that seems obvious but can be hard to define.[19] In turn, this makes it harder to measure it – to quantify or qualify it. Vagueness might not matter in everyday chats, but clarity is crucial for academic research and how we apply it. At its most basic, wellbeing is just feeling well – 'the experience of health, happiness and prosperity'. And this includes good mental health, life satisfaction, a sense of meaning in life, and how well we cope with stress.[20] It is useful to think of wellbeing as a state of balance (equilibrium). It is how well our personal resources meet our life challenges, in the physical, social, and psychological domains.[21]

From a research perspective, this helps to ensure that the research is relevant to the people taking part in the study. It is vital to keep in mind who will read the research and whom it seeks to benefit. This thought leads us to the aims and means of psychology.

What is psychology? What is research?

Academic psychology is evidence-based. It aims to explore, in a systematic way, what makes us tick and what it means to be human. It claims to be 'the scientific study of mind and behaviour'.[22] To realize this goal, we use methods from the natural sciences such as experiments, observations, and surveys. These methods give us data in the form of numbers (quantitative), or words and pictures (qualitative), or a mixture of both.[23] Conclusions are led by the data. We should not jump to them, or 'go beyond' the data. But it is also about more than just the data. It is about the spirit of science and the quest for ever-closer approximations to the truth.

Psychology aims to develop and test theories to uncover universal principles that explain and predict human behaviour and experience. Sometimes it confirms 'common sense' and, at others, it offers a radically different view. This gap can be jarring, especially when experts disagree with one another. But as playwright and poet Oscar Wilde said, 'The truth is rarely pure and never simple'.[24] Often, we cannot condense complex research findings to pithy newspaper headlines – without losing something vital. There are always caveats and footnotes. In the real world, when we crave certainty, this 'small print' can be annoying.[25] However, a more methodical approach can help to assess the various aspects of being human (and being well). We can seek to 'isolate'[26] the personal from the psychological and the cultural.[27] And each aspect will have a distinct back story, as we explore in the next chapter. Meanwhile, briefly, we look at the difference between academic psychology and pop psychology.

Bridging the knowledge gap

The Psychology of Wellbeing draws on a wealth of ideas, theories and evidence from a broad review of disciplines. Because rather than a fixed line between subjects, the boundaries are fuzzy.

So far, we have used the words 'psychology' and 'research' in an academic sense. Compared with pop psychology books, academic ones can feel 'dry and detached'. Usually, academic papers are written in the passive voice – from a third person perspective. It is because what is being done is more important than who is doing it. By contrast, pop psychology is more about the doer – the guru. Self-help texts are often punchier, are more directive, and seem 'more confident' and 'in your face'. Which is probably what makes them so popular![28]

Ideally, the use of scientific methods makes academic psychology a more cautious and conservative project. It is not geared towards scientific revolution but is more to do with small advances. It aims to be a collective aspiration of 'standing on the shoulders of giants'.[29] Research findings are scrutinized and reviewed by peers when published in journals. It is a slow process. Also, academic writing is an appeal to the intellect, while self-books, more likely, appeal to the emotions. Pop psychology authors might also refer to their 'research', but it is not always clear what this means. It could be a survey, a show-of-hands in their workshops, a collection of anecdotes, or a literature review. Their description of the research method might not be clear enough to allow someone to replicate it, which is vital in academia.

Conversely, an evidence-based, scientific approach to psychology is not immune from bias and error. This shortcoming is inevitable whenever people study people.[30] And, one way to pre-empt such bias is to approach research in a more reflexive way.[31] That is, we as researchers cite ourselves within the research. We say who we are and what we bring to the process. Our back story acts as a filter for everything we read and write. And, insights and assumptions change depending on 'the who, the what, the when, the where and the why'. These considerations can only lead us to ask better questions. These, in turn, will have an impact on how we read, write, and research wellbeing, and how we apply new understanding to take us forward to ask even better questions. And on it goes.

Nowadays, the distinction between academic psychology and pop psychology is blurred. If you visit a bookshop, you might see the same title in both sections. There are many excellent pop psychology books on the market – based on sound evidence. One of the aims of this book is to help you to spot them.

HOW THE STORY UNFOLDS IN THE REST OF THE BOOK

The adage for planning a talk or an essay states that in an introduction you 'tell 'em what you are going to tell 'em'. It is because context is essential to help us to process information. It helps us align new material with existing knowledge.[32] So, to ease that process, here is a run-down of the chapters that follow.

- Chapter 2 consider subjects of trust, truth, knowledge, and power and how they apply to wellbeing. It also gives a critical framework to establish the reliability of information sources.
- Chapter 3 builds on the core definitions and develops the idea of storytelling in psychology. It also develops the key definitions of wellbeing and the self, as well as looking at how inequality affects wellbeing.
- Chapter 4 looks at the modern-day scourge of stress and the psychological models used to explain it and help us to cope with it.
- Chapter 5 offers a critical review of the self-help industry and offers a plan of choosing and getting the most out of self-help books.
- Chapter 6 looks at models of wellbeing from positive psychology as well as criticisms and suggestions for ways forward.

Chapter 7 offers some concluding thoughts and a story to pull together the themes of the book. The book ends with a return to self-reflection and offers story to structure your wellbeing goals.

SUMMARY AND REFLECTION

This introduction has:

- set the scene for the debate on wellbeing and offered basic working definitions of key terms (psychology, the self, wellbeing, and research).
- put forward the concepts of reflection and storytelling as a starting point for critical analysis.
- outlined the plan for the rest of the book.

Before reading on, reflect on how this chapter has affected your thoughts on wellbeing and what questions it has provoked.

The next chapter considers a framework to check the reliability of information sources and establish trust.

2

QUESTIONS OF TRUST
The truth about wellbeing

TOO MUCH INFORMATION

We live in a 'message-dense' world in the age of 'over-communication'. In these times it can be 'difficult to devote the mental energy necessary to make sense of . . . the important issues of the day'.[1] In times of stress and anxiety, some higher-level cognitive functions switch off.[2] It becomes harder to process information. So anything that cuts down on time and cognitive resources appeals to us. That's why 'skim reading' has become the new norm. But although it helps us to grasp the headlines, we often overlook the small print.[3]

We all have our trusted 'go-to' news and information sources, and ones we 'avoid like the plague'. And we use trust as a filter to help make sense of a complex world. Psychologist Ken Rotenberg goes as far as to argue that 'trust is the cornerstone of society and essential to its survival'.[4] But it seems many of us have 'trust issues'. According to *Edelman's 2020 Trust Barometer*, in the UK, two thirds (67%) worry that technology will make it impossible to know if what we are seeing, or hearing, is real![5]

In this chapter, we explore issues around sense-making and the pursuit of truth and the effects of post-truth and fake news. It looks at the relationship between trust, politics, news, and wellbeing. It also considers how the COVID-19 pandemic has affected our attitudes to wellness. The chapter ends with a review of the 'obstacles to knowledge' and questions we can use to guide reading and research.

TRUST, TRUTH, POST-TRUTH, AND ANYTHING BUT THE TRUTH

Every TV courtroom drama features the solemn promise 'to tell the truth, the whole truth, and nothing but the truth'. And it ends with the appeal 'so help me God'. Also, the motto of the United States of America is 'In God We Trust'. It's a simple model where truth and trust go hand in hand. But faith in religion has declined, certainly in the West, with a shift to a more humanistic-values-based outlook. And traditional religious views have not kept pace with more liberal social attitudes.[6] Now in this digital age, we are bombarded with multiple versions of the truth, told from different angles. This shift is highlighted in Neil Gaiman's fantasy novel *American Gods*. It is a blend of ancient and modern mythology that tells the tale of the battle for sovereignty between the gods of old religions and the 'new gods'.[7] These new gods are avatars of technology, such as media, the stock market, and globalization. And the 'spooks' – the intelligence agents – of the new gods are the materialized beliefs in conspiracy theories.

In a post-truth world, feelings trump facts. Or rather, the choice of facts to explain the world is led by emotion. And, lies can be rebranded as 'alternative facts' to fit our versions of the truth. Put simply, 'If it feels right, it's true. Or at least, true enough'.[8]

Back in the 'real' world, 'old-school' faith in religion has declined in the West.[9] But trust in the 'new gods' has taken a hit too. According to *Edelman's 2020 Trust Barometer*,[10] in the UK:

- Three in five (60%) people worry that the pace of technology is too fast.
- More than seven in ten (72%) people report that the government does not understand emerging technologies enough to regulate them effectively.

- More than seven in ten (72%) worry about false information or fake news being used as a weapon.
- Three in five (60%) believe politicians are purposely using public policy issues to create an environment of fear that they can exploit for political gain.

Edelman asserts that we grant our trust based on two factors: *competence* and *ethical behaviour*. For competence, we assess how well people and organizations deliver on their promises. And, for ethics, whether they do the right thing for the improvement of society. Notably, in the survey, governments are rated the least competent and least ethical. The mass media do not fare much better. Businesses are rated slightly unethical and slightly competent, and non-governmental organizations (NGOs) are moderately ethical, albeit lacking in competence. So why does there seem to be a crisis of trust?

Crisis? What crisis?

In 2015's *Trust Barometer*, Edelman links the fall in trust to the failures of governments and institutions to show leadership and give answers in major crises – humanitarian, health, security, and financial. Examples include the refugee crisis, data breaches, stock market downturns, Ebola, and corruption scandals.[11] And, the novel coronavirus pandemic has also raised questions of trust in politicians. Both UK and US efforts have been marked by denial, dither, delay, mixed messages, strategy changes, and spin. At the start of 2020, when Chinese scientists raised alarm bells in about the novel coronavirus, the UK government was crowdfunding for 'Big Ben Bongs' for Brexit![12] Both the UK and the US lost time with their first response to COVID-19, compared to the actions of Asian countries. South Korea adopted a track, trace, and treat policy, whereas the UK opted for a 'herd immunity' approach.[13] In the UK, early in the crisis, the government came under pressure to publish the data and the model used for its approach. Dr Richard Horton, editor-in-chief of *The*

Lancet, argued, 'This transparency is essential to retain the scientific community, healthcare community, and the public's understanding, co-operation and trust'.[14] A lack of trust led to conspiracy theories, suspicion, and confusion between nations.[15] And, we cannot disregard the machismo of some leaders that impeded teamwork. It's the same script used to deal with other global problems, such as pollution and climate change.[16]

Sociologists Raewyn Connell and Rebecca Pearse argue that gender has a social and relational impact that extends nationally, and internationally, to economies, states, and global relations.[17] We can see gender stereotypes at work in handling the COVID-19 crisis among leaders. Where women-led countries have had better outcomes. The 'cardinal pillars of masculinity' are easy to spot, that is, the need, at all costs, to be superior, independent, and the most powerful.[18] The key message is a 'prove you're a man' or 'die trying'and take every one down with you!

How governments have managed the pandemic shines a light on how we, as individuals, deal with health and wellbeing problems.

Just what the doctor ordered

A national survey in the US found four main themes for reasons to avoid seeking medical care. These are low perceived need, traditional barriers, unfavourable evaluations, and personality traits.[19]

- *Low perceived need*: 'it'll improve over time', 'it's not that serious', or prefers spiritual healing or natural remedies.
- *Traditional barriers*: being too busy, taking time off work, and the costs (if no national healthcare provision). Also, childcare, language barriers, mobility issues, and mental health conditions.
- *Unfavourable evaluations*: a general dislike of doctors, lack of trust, and a dislike of doctors' communication styles. Also, fear of a serious diagnosis, fear of embarrassing procedures, and guilt about unhealthy behaviours.
- *Personality traits*: such as laziness, procrastination, stubbornness, and forgetfulness.

The first three themes define the delayed response to the coronavirus pandemic: 'it's just the flu', 'think of the economy and the disruption', and 'what do experts know, anyway?'

However, once a person visits the doctor, there is a ream of psychological justifications for ignoring medical advice. Medical doctor Alex Lickerman offers two reasons he hears from patients who refuse medical treatment. The first is that people often believe stories more than they believe the evidence. A story from a friend, or a friend of a friend, is more compelling than abstract statistics on outcomes. And second that outcomes are rarely black and white, such as balancing the illness with side effects of the treatment.[20] Then the reasons that caused us to avoid medical care, in the first place, come into play. On top of which we have cognitive biases. We might not like what we hear, and we think we know more than medical experts do. Also, some might feel that to follow a treatment plan is a loss of power, a sign of weakness or an admission of defeat.[21] Mood and emotion also play a part. When we are angry, we are less likely to take advice. Men are more likely than women to underestimate the longer-term complications associated with health problems. Another obstacle is difficulty in changing habits and behaviours, or a dislike of being tied to a routine. An imposed health regimen might also clash with a person's sense of self as carefree and spontaneous. But overall, if we seek advice in a spirit of cooperation and in partnership with professionals, it helps to foster positive emotions and build trust and makes us more likely to use the information.[22]

These findings show that our relationship with trust is more complicated than a combination of competence and ethics. It is mediated by our sense of self, our needs, attitudes, and circumstances. Developmental psychologist Erik Erikson defines 'basic trust' as a general sense of the correspondence between one's needs and one's world, while 'basic mistrust is a readiness for danger or an anticipation of discomfort'.[23] Trust is pivotal to our wellbeing – that is, how well our personal resources meet our life challenges.[24] In short, our decision to seek and accept medical advice is based on whether we trust it to make things better or worse. And this brings us back to notions of 'the truth' and how we make decisions in a post-truth age.

WHEN THE FACTS GET IN THE WAY
OF THE STORY

Conspiracy-theories-a-go-go

In 2018 the BBC conceded it got the coverage of climate change wrong 'too often'. And in its quest for balanced coverage, it sometimes breaches its own editorial guidelines and broadcasting rules. In a briefing note to all staff, it warned of 'false balance' and that 'to achieve impartiality you do not need to include outright deniers' of global warming.[25] Although the BBC has learned this lesson, other media outlets have not.

During the COVID-19 pandemic, the 'conspiracy-theory mill' went into overdrive. And the UK government's new anti-fake-news 'rapid response unit' had to deal with ten bogus articles a day. In one case, a false report had more views than all those posted by the National Health Service (NHS) put together.[26] An item on one ultra-right-wing US website got over 160,000 engagements by UK users in 24 hours.[27] And the UK's broadcasting regulatory *Ofcom* warned media outlets that they would face sanctions if they give airtime to false health advice about coronavirus. This warning came after a radio station featured a guest introduced as a 'registered nurse' who promoted the coronavirus/5G conspiracy theory. During the 20-minute interview, the guest launched an attack on health professionals in the NHS dealing with the pandemic.[28] Her speech is worth quoting at length:

> Just because you have this qualification, do not wear that like a crown of glory. . . . The days are gone when you were a doctor and a nurse and everybody trusted you. Those days are well gone. Do your own research. Do not trust a qualification. . . . Because remember the people that own the establishments that teach us, it all travels back to the same thing. It's all owned by big pharma. They own the medical elite and they determine what gets published.

Conspiracy theories have a viral quality. Believing in one increases the likelihood that others will be accepted.[29] Although there are important points in her discourse, such as 'do your own research', it depends how you define research and how you have been trained to do it, if at all.

Mixed messages – emotion and objectivity

Social media and digital devices have changed how we understand and engage with news output.[30] We now feel more invested and involved. News stories routinely use on-the-spot footage from mobile (cell) phones. We also interact with journalists on social media and contribute content. The director of journalism think tank *Polis*, Professor Charlie Beckett, calls this 'networked journalism' where 'the audience is now part of the process'. To keep engagement, in competition with other media, he argues that there is a trend towards a more 'personalised and emotionally-driven news media'. He also says that this shift is 'redefining the classic idea of journalistic objectivity, indeed, it is reshaping the idea of news itself'. Beckett's argument for a reflexive journalism is like the idea of a more reflexive approach to psychology. He calls for structure based on evidence and reason, but one where there is room for subjectivity. Otherwise, 'if everything is subjective then nothing is false, and nothing is true'. He maintains that it is still 'the job of journalism (and psychology) to challenge cognitive bias not to reinforce it'. For Beckett, 'the key principle in this – for the citizen as well as the journalist – is transparency', and he contends that 'transparency is the new objectivity'.[31]

The transition between the old and new paradigms has not been smooth. It sometimes looks like a chapter from the video game *Assassin's Creed* where 'Nothing is true, everything is permitted'.[32] In short, a post-truth, 'free-for-all' of blurred boundaries and ambiguity, where conspiracy theorists get a platform, because to deny them one would feel like censorship.[33] Or, risk the ire of online trolls who look to exert editorial control, often using abusive tactics, especially to female journalists. Or, those making 'constructive' comments about how journalists should present themselves, such as clothing and hairstyle choices.[34] In this 'feels-true-enough' era, journalists head to Twitter without double-checking their scoops.[35]

The unreliable narrator

During the run-up to the 2019 UK general election, amidst accusations of media bias,[36] writer, poet, and broadcaster Michael Rosen tweeted, 'When we study English we are alerted to the idea of the "unreliable narrator". Strangely, the media seem unaware of this idea'.[37] Examples of the unreliable narrator in books (and films) include *Catcher in the Rye*, *Fight Club*, *The Sixth Sense*, and *Shutter Island*.[38] These stories rely on our trust in the narrator's version of the truth. Throughout, there are hints that all is not as it seems. The twist comes at the end when the fallacy is revealed. So, Rosen's comment is another way of saying that in the eagerness to 'tell its story', the media had neglected to interrogate the reliability of its 'witnesses'.

The journalist and broadcaster Peter Oborne goes further. In an interview with Channel Four News, he accused media out-lets of 'debauching political discourse' and spreading 'fake news' on behalf of the UK government.[39] It's noteworthy that Oborne has worked for right-wing newspapers such as *The Telegraph* and *The Daily Mail*.[40] He argues, 'Instead of doing the job of a journalist, which is to interrogate in a sceptical way the information you're getting . . . what they are actually doing is shovelling it on unme-diated'. Oborne contends that this creates two versions of the truth – one from the official press office view and the other from 'unnamed senior sources' which contain fake news yet is reported uncritically.[41]

There's an often-cited saying about balance in the media. It goes, 'If someone says it's raining, and another person says it's dry, it's not your job to quote them both. Your job is to look out the fucking win-dow and find out which is true'. The only attribution I could find was Jonathan Foster, senior lecturer in journalism studies and reporter. So, I wrote to him.[42] He confirms that the quotation is a composite of a journalism skills module taught by him and a colleague. But he stressed that neither of them would have said, 'it's your job to look out of the window'. It's a great quote but anyone who uses it would do well to remember Oscar Wilde's famous epigram, 'Don't believe everything you read on the Internet'.[43]

In a speech to veterans in 2018, President Donald Trump uttered a line you might find in a dystopian novel. He said, 'Just remember, what you are seeing and what you are reading is not what's happening. Just stick with us, don't believe the crap you see from these people, the fake news'.[44] The message is, in an age of distrust, 'trust no one, don't trust the evidence of your senses; trust me'.[45]

Fake news: faster than the speed of truth

There is worldwide concern over fake news and how it might influence political, economic, and social wellbeing.[46] Although made popular by President Donald Trump since 2017, the term 'fake news' has been around since the end of the 19th century.[47] It is a vague term that conflates a range of false information, from genuine error or shoddy journalism, to parody and satire to malign content. In official papers, the UK government prefers the term 'misinformation' or 'disinformation', depending on the perceived goal.[48] 'It can be used to provoke, to arouse passion, to profit, for political influence, and 'propaganda''.[49] Trump uses it against negative mainstream press coverage he receives; that is, anything he doesn't like.[50] And, during the 2019 general election campaign in the UK, 88% of advertisements were found to be misleading, including false claims about the NHS. Some also contained links to webpages that included false claims.[51]

False information is also used for profit, most notably from social media advertising. Often bogus health cures – using cancer as a trigger word – get hundreds of thousands of engagements. One tactic they use are urgent calls to action that tap into our fear of missing out. These might include conspiracy type by-lines such as the threat of censorship and the plans by social media platforms to label the story 'fake-news'.[52] Early in the COVID-19 crisis, the director-general of the

World Health Organization (WHO), Tedros Adhanom Ghebreyesus, warned, 'We're not just fighting an epidemic; we're fighting an "infodemic". Fake news spreads faster and more easily than this virus and is just as dangerous'.[53]

Data scientists at the Massachusetts Institute of Technology (MIT) in a paper for *Science* looked at how and why true and false news stories spread differently. They used a data set of 126,000 of 'rumour cascades' on Twitter from 2006 to 2017. The rumours were tweeted by 3 million people, a total of 4.5 million times.[54] The researchers found that false news travelled faster and reached more people than did the truth. So, while true stories rarely reached over 1,000 people, the false news reached between 1,000 and 10,000. But why? Well, they found that novelty value and emotional reaction played a part. False news is often novel, and novel information is more likely to be retweeted. Emotionally, false news is most likely to provoke surprise, fear, and disgust. True news is met with sadness, joy, anticipation, and trust. And false political news reached more people faster than did any other false information.[55]

In a 2017 talk to Google staff, Noam Chomsky, cognitive scientist and social critic, was asked the question, 'How do you think Google can and should handle the fake news problem?' He replied, 'Well, by not contributing to it'.[56] John Naughton, professor of the public understanding of technology, argues that we need something analogous to 'social distancing' for social media false news.[57] Fake news goes viral because people spread it. So, when faced with a tweet that both surprises you and arouses strong negative emotions, put in some cognitive distance. Don't react to the emotion trigger. Think first and check the facts.

DOING IT BY THE BOOK

In her song 'Same Time Tomorrow', performance artist Laurie Anderson says when we're told to do something 'by the book', we have to ask, 'What book?' She adds, 'because it would make a big difference if it was Dostoyevski or just . . . Ivanhoe'.[58] Now, these two seemingly random choices are apt for the quest for the truth in a post-truth age of fake news and 'alternative facts'. *Ivanhoe*, written by Walter Scott, is a romantic tale of knights, chivalry, outlaws, and witch trials set in 12th-century England. Fyodor Dostoevsky was a Russian novelist and philosopher. And his works explored human psychology in the 'troubled political, social, and spiritual atmospheres'. His works feature 'portrayals of intellectuals, who "feel ideas" in the depths of their souls'.[59]

A contemporary example can help to illustrate the tension between feelings and intellect in decision-making around issues of health and wellbeing.

Cuts both ways

The reality TV show *Botched* features people's experiences of failed cosmetic procedures – often at the hands of unqualified, cut-price 'surgeons'.[60] The most common reasons for choosing a surgeon are based on word-of mouth recommendations. And many say they did their own research. But mostly, their choices are economic ones – they want premium results for bargain prices.[61] Despite disastrous results and against their better judgement, they went back for revisions and corrections.[62] Elective cosmetic surgery is an emotional decision. And it is one, often, where physical changes are sought to improve psychological wellbeing. The reasons for seeking surgery include low self-ratings on self-esteem, life satisfaction, and attractiveness. For men, the reasons include low body image satisfaction and stress linked to the masculine gender role.[63] For both women and men, greater mass media and social networking sites are named as influences to seek cosmetic procedures. For adolescents, in particular, the adoration and psychological attachment to celebrities is related to greater acceptance of plastic surgery.[64]

In contrast, the guidelines from professional bodies focus on patient safety and informed consent. They stress the importance of taking time to decide, checking qualifications and accreditations, and asking questions. Feelings and common sense play a part, but after the facts, not as a filter through which we collect facts. Guidelines also stress the importance of getting all the practical details such as time and location. They also have warnings about 'free' consultations or the pressure of 'special offers' or any other inducements. And finally, people should look for professional guidelines which stress that a patients can change their minds.[65]

Let's consider the sense-making process in more detail.

Bridging the knowledge gap

To 'do things by the book', I went back to the ideas of Roger Bacon, the 13th-century philosopher, popularly known as 'Dr Mirabilis'. He was an extraordinary scholar, a polymath whose work spanned mathematics, astronomy, optics, alchemy, and languages. But it is his thoughts on scientific knowledge which helps to enlighten the call to 'do your own research'. He proposes two levels of understanding.[66]

Intuition

The first level is an innate, implicit knowledge that he describes as 'imperfect and confused' but 'inclined toward the truth'.[67] Think of this as 'sense-making through automatic, intuitive processes' important for survival. This includes our ability to perceive patterns and to detect agency in others. And it helps us to predict the consequences of our behaviour.[68] But this ability to 'join the dots' is flawed. Sometimes it sees patterns and relationships in random or chance occurrences. It can also ascribe agency to the actions of others in error. Notably, conspiracy theories include complex plans that involve many agents[69] – 'they are all in it together'.

Research has shown that a greater focus on emotion and a lesser emphasis on reflective thinking leads to an increase in belief in false news content.[70] And, one of the perils of 'armchair psychology' is confirmation bias – the tendency to cherry pick those data. It creates an 'echo chamber' in response to emotional triggers that that we only want to hear views that support our views and confirm our prejudgements.[71] But if we are to step outside our 'filter bubble', we must ask questions.

Experimentation

At the second level, Bacon puts explicit rational knowledge. One part is 'the knowledge of the principles of science' and the other 'the knowledge of conclusions'. So rather than saying 'everyone is entitled to their opinion', Bacon talks about our 'right to investigate'. He proclaimed, 'It is the credo of free men this opportunity to try, this privilege to err, this courage to experiment anew. We scientists of the human spirit shall experiment, experiment, ever experiment'.

In its simplest sense 'experiment' means 'a test done in order to learn something or to discover if something works or is true'.[72]The key phrase here is 'to discover if'. Philosopher Friedrich Nietzsche writes, 'The thinker sees in his own actions, attempts, and questionings to obtain information about something or other; success and failure are answers to him first and foremost'.[73] And the 'privilege of trial and error', at the heart of the scientific process, can lead to a lack of trust – the idea that experts can't agree or come up with definite answers. *Edelman's Trust Barometer* found that people are more likely to trust the applications of science, rather than science itself.[74] In other words, we trust the concrete over the abstract.

The Dunning-Kruger effect goes some way to tell us why some have a low opinion of experts. It's a cognitive bias that explains why some people overestimate their reasoning abilities – that is, how smart they are. People in the bottom quartile tend to see themselves as more mid-range, while the highest quartile tends to slightly underestimate their abilities. At the third quartile (above average but not at the top) tend to have an accurate idea of their abilities. It lends support to the popular notion that 'the more you know the more you realize what you don't know'. So, people in the lowest quartile tend to be overconfident in their abilities and overlook their own mistakes or lack of skill. They also do not recognize the skill and expertise of others.[75] For some, the cautious and conservative tone might add to the impression that 'experts are not to be trusted'.

So how do we make sense of it all?

OBSTACLES TO KNOWLEDGE

To look forward, we go back to 'first principles' of how to 'do' science. Roger Bacon, in his *Opus Majus*, proposes four obstacles to 'grasping truth'.[76] They apply to academic psychology, common knowledge, and pop psychology alike. They are:

1 Submission to unworthy or unsuited authority.
2 Influence of custom.
3 Popular prejudice, or the opinion of the unlearned crowd.
4 Concealment of our ignorance through ostentatious displays of our apparent wisdom.

Submission to unworthy or unsuited authority

As the saying goes, 'we are all judged by the company we keep'. Although this is not always true of people, it is for arguments. So, 'our arguments are judged by the authorities we cite'. Various translations on Bacon's text replace 'unworthy' and 'unsuited' with 'weak, unreliable or faulty'.[77] Therefore, his first obstacle to grasping truth is about the trust we place in our sources. Who are these experts?

It helps to define 'expert' in a general sense by thinking of expert witnesses in court cases. The role of the expert is to give an unbiased and objective opinion within the area of their expertise. And to be a worthy expert, they must prove qualifications, relevant experience, and accreditation and give details of information used to make their statement.[78] In *Edelman's Trust Barometer*, trust was higher for academic scientists compared to those working in commercial settings. There's a sense that academic science is more neutral in its goals. And it's customary in academic papers to declare competing interests and funding.

Beware of self-proclaimed sceptics and 'alternative' viewpoints. There is a difference between the scepticism valued by science and 'pseudo-scepticism'. A warning sign that you have stumbled on a pseudo-sceptics site is the language they use. Scientists may disagree with each other's findings, but they won't use words like 'claptrap' or trade insults. These are signs of emotional appeals, not rational arguments. The same standards of conduct and practice should apply.[79]

Influence of custom

A custom is 'a usage or practice common to many or to a particular place or class or habitual with an individual'.[80] For instance, it is customary among psychology students to include 'gender differences' in research projects without questioning why and if it makes sense. Also, when working as a research consultant on social policy projects, the habitual response in the organizations is 'we need a survey' – even when the sample size is small and percentages are meaningless. Customs and habits are the things we do without thinking. The COVID-19 crisis, for example, has caused us to rethink our taken-for-granted assumptions. Greeting people, personal space, and how to wash our hands have all come under scrutiny. And how we produce knowledge has changed with more international cooperation and fast-tracked publications. We found a better way once we stopped letting custom dictate.

Popular prejudice, or the opinion of the unlearned crowd

Whenever you hear 'as everyone knows', it is a cue to ask if what follows is a universal truth. Also, the phrase 'it's only common sense' might not be about 'sense' at all, but instead an appeal to popular feeling. Academic psychology contradicts the common-sense view more often than we'd expect.

Common sense

Radio talk show host Dennis Prager (in the US) claims, 'there are two kinds of studies in the world: those that confirm your common sense, and those that are wrong'.[81] But it's an appeal to trust intuition over rational processes. There's an unspoken assumption that 'common sense' and 'free speech' belong together and the belief that common sense is value-free. But in 2017, Prager sued Google for putting his 'educational' YouTube videos into restricted mode. Google considered the themes to be more suitable for a mature audience.[82] So here are two quite different definitions both of common sense and of free speech.

Yes, one aspect of Prager's argument does make common sense and rational sense. He states, 'whenever you hear the words "studies show" . . . and these studies show the opposite of what common sense suggests, be very sceptical'.[83] And he's right. But the opposite is also true. When 'common sense' claims the monopoly on the truth, be very sceptical. Prager's intuitive approach is to ignore the studies. The rational approach is to ask, 'what studies?' Because when someone says 'studies show' but cannot cite them, the phrase is as hollow, as 'everybody knows'.

I'm entitled to my opinion

Science fiction writer Isaac Asimov wrote a provocative article called 'A Cult of Ignorance'. In it, he argues, 'anti-intellectualism has been a constant thread winding its way through our political and cultural life, nurtured by the false notion that democracy means that "my ignorance is just as good as your knowledge" '.[84] In everyday speech, we hear, 'It's a free country; I'm entitled to my opinion'. But as philosophy scholar Sandy Goldberg argues, having a legal and political right to express an argument does not validate it. Freedom to express one's beliefs and being able to back them up with evidence are two different things. The latter is 'epistemically warranted' – which means it is based on adequate reasons and grounded in evidence.[85] Or to use

Roger Bacon's term, 'explicit rational knowledge'. On this view, 'you are only entitled to what you can argue for'. To use a retail analogy, we should trust the product's warranty more than a stranger's opinion.

Popularity over accuracy

Social media usage and misinformation surged during the COVID-19 pandemic include dangerous advice on how to combat the virus. And in the rush to share information, many do not check if it is true. People with greater science knowledge and who used more analytical thinking are more astute in what they share. Even just a simple 'nudge' to pause and think about the accuracy reduces the spread of false information.[86] And even better if you verify the information on a fact-checking website.[87] However, sharing the truth is often not the main motivation on social media. On Twitter, people share to show approval, to argue, to get attention, or to entertain and amuse.[88]

The bigger picture

Traditionally, psychology has used a convenient population to test its theories – White, middle-class (often male) students. The quest for universal truths left out large sections of the population from the bigger picture.[89] Psychology has unconsciously (or consciously) imported biases from the 'real world'. But it started to change when researchers asked better questions. When we talk about 'mind, behaviour and experience' in psychology, we need to ask 'whose'? Are Black, Asian, and Minority Ethnic (BAME) voices and experiences represented? Have we included people with disabilities?[90]

Feminist psychology challenged and changed traditional ways of 'knowledge-making', including the subject matter of psychology and the methods used to collect evidence. This paved the way for LGBTQI+ perspectives. But this is often not the case in pop psychology. Self-help books on relationships and gender offer a 'one-size-fits-all' definition man and woman, into which we must force ourselves into Procrustean-style, if the books are to make sense.

Concealment of our ignorance through ostentatious displays of our apparent wisdom

When writing essays, students often make the mistake that 'to be clever you must write clever'. And, in my study skills workshops, I urge them to let go of this idea. So, rather than 'promulgating their esoteric cogitations', I urge them to 'make known their deepest thoughts'. That is, don't use big words.[91] Academic books can be dense and opaque, and they see this as the 'gold standard'. Sociologist Stanislav Andreski is highly critical of social scientists who 'manipulate through description' and hide behind a 'smokescreen of jargon'.[92] Politician and biographer Boris Johnson explains in his biography of Winston Churchill the secret of a great orator. He argues that it is in the choice of simple Anglo-Saxon words over Latinate ones.[93] Churchill disliked 'unnecessarily long and flowery words' and 'bureaucratic jargon'.[94] Johnson also offers an insight into the world of politics and warns that when a politician uses more Latinate words, it is often an attempt, on their part, to obscure gaps in the argument.

According to plain language expert Deborah S. Bosley, 'traditionally, academics didn't write with the public or the average person in mind. They wrote to impress their peers'.[95] But more recently, with an emphasis on public engagement, the goal is to write in a more accessible way. So, in study skills coaching, I recommend students pitch their essays to a well-informed 14 year-old.[96] Then, there's no place to hide, and the arguments 'stand out'.

This leads us to how knowledge is created and what it is used for.

WHAT IS THIS KNOWLEDGE OF WHICH YOU SPEAK?

As storytelling is a main theme in this book, it helps to think like a historian when sourcing information (and passing it on). Is it relevant, useful, and reliable? Can you trust it? Here are five factors that will help you to decide.[97]

- *Origin*: Whose knowledge is it? Is it evidence-based research? Is it a first-hand account? Who made it? How was it made?
- *Perspective*: From what point of view was the knowledge created? How does this source corroborate contradict information from other sources?
- *Context*: When and where was the source created? What events and conditions are important for the creation of the knowledge?
- *Audience*: Who was the knowledge made for?
- *Motive*: For what purpose was the knowledge made? What's the motive for passing it on? Was it to inform or to influence? Why has it been made this way? Whose interests is it serving?

The phrase 'knowledge is power' is embedded in our consciousness. Psychologists Wendy and Rex Stainton-Rogers offer a series of questions to challenge knowledge and power, some of which have been included above. I have combined politician Tony Benn's five essential questions of democracy[98] to give four factors to explore.

- *Authority*: By whose authority was the knowledge made? Where did they get the power or authority to make it? To whom are the knowledge-makers accountable? How can we check or challenge that authority?
- *Emphasis*: What does the knowledge include and emphasize and what does it omit, exclude, or obscure?
- *Effects*: What happens because of it? Who benefits from it and who loses?
- *Alternatives*: What would happen if different knowledge were accepted?

These nine factors offer an antidote in a post-truth age, so that we can assess information around health and wellbeing beyond its emotional attraction.

BUT DOES TRUST MATTER IN MATTERS OF WELLBEING?

Being less trusting might seem a good survival strategy, but research shows that it impacts negatively on psychological and physical health. People without generalized trust in others tend to be more cynical, to lack social support, and are less willing to seek medical treatment when needed. They also tend to have shorter lives. On the other hand, patients who work in partnership with health providers and are better informed tend to enjoy better health. Working alliances, shared decision making, and trust are associated with greater satisfaction, being more likely to stick to treatment plans, and improved patient outcomes.[99] Knowledge is empowerment.

SUMMARY AND REFLECTION

In this chapter we:

- explored the themes of trust, truth, post-truth and transparency included fake news and these might impact on health and wellbeing.
- examined the difference between opinion and knowledge
- considered a framework to overcome obstacles to knowledge and how to interrogate information sources.

What insights has this chapter sparked for you about how you gather information to make decisions about health and wellbeing issues?

The next chapter further explores the idea of storytelling and how we use it to make sense of the world.

3

STORYTELLING AND
SENSE-MAKING

50 shades of wellbeing

Every mundane enquiry about health and wellbeing is an invitation
to tell a story.

> 'How are you today?'
> 'Okay. Fine, thanks, can't complain, and you?'
> 'Yes. Not so bad. Mustn't crumble', laughs and adds 'I mean grumble'.

That's a story. It's a short one, but it's a story all the same. Because
what we leave out is as important as what we put in, sometimes more
so. In British culture, when friends give a terse response to questions
about their wellness, we probe a little more. Especially if we sense
they are not telling us 'the whole story'. We might ask, 'Yes, but how
are you in yourself?' It's an odd but profound question. It goes to the
heart of psychological wellbeing – the subjective experience of being
well in your self.

Reflect for a moment on the opening dialogue. Even based on this
brief encounter, you could create a back story for each of the characters. Because as sense-makers, we 'join the dots', read between the
lines, and fill in the gaps. So, what do you think is going on? Are they
just too busy to chat? Or are they just being polite and 'going through

the motions'? Are they happy? Are they well 'in themselves'? Or is there something else beneath the surface civility? And how do you know?

In this chapter, we consider what psychologist Theodore Sarbin calls 'the storied nature of human conduct' – narrative psychology.[1] It forms the basis of a framework to assess approaches to wellness – from academic to pop psychology to 'common sense' views. We expand on our working definition of 'the self' and wellbeing as we explore the psychology of 'making sense' and how we manage beliefs, knowledge, and understanding. Also, how do our shades of experience – from the personal to the social to the political – colour our wellbeing stories?

STORIES WE LIVE BY

It is tempting to dismiss storytelling as mere entertainment. If asked to name a great storyteller, you might say William Shakespeare, Walt Disney, Maya Angelou, or J.K. Rowling. Or maybe, for you, it's the classic fairy tales of the Brothers Grimm or Hans Christian Andersen. These lists are stories in themselves. They say something about us. I know I'm less likely to cite the incredibly prolific Ishtiaq Ahmad and more likely to list authors whose books form part of my autobiography, like Oscar Wilde, James Baldwin, Antoine de Saint-Exupéry, and Jean Cocteau. Who's on your list?

Storytelling is much more than novels and fairy tales and entertainment; it's at the heart of our psychology. Writer and story coach Lisa Cron sums up its importance in two lines. She writes, 'Storytelling . . . was crucial to our evolution – more so than opposable thumbs. Opposable thumbs let us hang on; story told us what to hang on to'.[2] We have been telling stories before we could write and before we could speak. From the beginning, we used them to plan, to develop social conventions, and to connect with others. And we still do. Early cultural accounts of how the universe came about – cosmologies – helped people to make sense of the universe and their place in it. They imposed a structure on roles, functions, attitudes, and relationships to those in the group and to outsiders.[3] Philosopher and author A.C. Grayling writes, 'philosophies that capture the imagination never wholly fade'.[4] And this certainly applies to Judaeo-Christian scripture, which literary scholar Elaine Scarry credits with 'sponsoring a civilization to a degree shared by no other isolated verbal text'. Its influence is, today, detectable in Western psychology, psychiatry, medicine, and the law.[5]

According to literary scholar and poet Barbara Hardy, all of us are natural storytellers, day and night devising our 'fictions and chronicles'. According to her, all aspects of human sense-making are narrative forms. She contends, 'we dream in narrative, daydream in narrative, remember, anticipate, hope, despair, believe, doubt, plan, revise, criticise, construct, gossip, learn, hate and love by narrative'.[6] Author and poet Michael Rosen writes that our 'stories are a currency with special secrets and significance' we use 'to position ourselves in the world. Even in simple exchanges about wellbeing, as we swap stories, we generalize and discover themes as "[y]our story triggers my story"'.[7] And, according to psychologist Ian Parker, 'everyday accounts of action and experience are the source of theories in psychology and these theories trickle back out from the discipline into the explanations that people give of themselves and their lives'.[8]

In narrative psychology, your life story is not just a serial account of life events. It's not just about what happened; it's about the way you weave the tale. In a cartoon Internet 'meme', one person behind a desk says, 'So, tell me a bit about yourself', and the other person replies, 'I'd rather not. I really need this job'.[9] Your autobiography is both less than and more than the facts. It both reveals and conceals who you are.[10] At interviews and on first dates we aim to present our best side – to 'sell' ourselves. It's our marketing 'signature story' – 'a strategic message' that 'clarifies or enhances the brand', makes sense of the past and sets our vision of the future. These stories exercise a pull over our actions, feelings, and choices.[11] According to psychologists Dan McAdams and Erika Manczak, 'Life stories do not simply reflect personality', they are an important part of our personality.[12]

Crucially, we don't tell our stories in isolation. They are contextually bound. And we often borrow and cherry-pick from existing cultural scripts which we edit to construct the ongoing story of who we are. But, as we share them, they become subject to 'critical analysis' and alternative readings. Sociologist Michael Mulkay argues, 'every "social interaction" and every "cultural product" or "text" has to be treated as a source or an opportunity for creating multiple meanings and further texts'.[13] We can see this in the more extreme aspects of online 'call-out culture',[14] where a line of text or even single words are taken out of context to create new texts. The original context, authorship, and intention become irrelevant as the new story prevails.[15] In this way, ours stories and our sense of self can get hijacked. And there's no benefit of the doubt in the binaries of the digital world. But no story or soundbite is an analogue of life itself. And instead of the knee-jerk reaction of 'hate first; think later' we need to take the time to listen. Because our 'critiques' of other people's stories often reveal far more about us than about the original texts.

YOU SAY SCHEMATA . . . LET'S CALL THE WHOLE THING OFF

In her book On Looking: Eleven Walks with Expert Eyes, cognitive psychologist Alexandra Horowitz takes a series of walks, along the same route, with a range of experts. Her companions include a sociologist, an artist, a geologist, a physician, and a sound engineer. She also walked with a dog and with a child.[16] Their accounts are markedly different. Horowitz reported that most of her fellow walkers reproached themselves for 'not paying good enough attention'.[17] The book shows that how we view the world is mediated by our sense of self, our culture, and our experience, expertise, and attitudes.

It is not possible to process afresh or store every bit of data that comes our way. Many routine situations do not need full analysis, just automatic responses. So, for cognitive economy, our pattern-seeking brains use structures (schemata) to reduce the load and focus our attention on what matters most to us.[18] Schemata (singular schema) are templates of ideas and routines. We can think of them as 'brain apps'.[19] Steeped in our culture, we cultivate them from birth, through our social interactions, experiences, and observations. These mental structures hold preconceived ideas about an aspect of the world. They help to 'smooth' our experience of the world, like cookies on websites. We have one schema for making a cup of tea, one for going to a restaurant, one to tell bedtime stories, and one to manage questions and access reliable information about wellbeing.

We have schemata about categories of information, our identity (self), other people, social roles, and how to behave in different situations. So, 'how-are-you' questions trigger a schema and going out to eat triggers another. Both will include options for a 'fast-food-I'm-fine-thanks' interaction or a 'three-course-a-la-carte-have-I-got a-tale-of-woe-to-tell-you'. Our schemata are both driven by our attitudes and reinforce our attitudes – our likes and dislikes, our values, our self-image.[20] And, as mentioned in Chapter 2, who or what we trust. Together, they provide frameworks to organize knowledge, focus our attention, filter our perceptions, shape memories, and plug the gaps with the most-likely-default values. Schemata smooth out our experiences, forecast likely events, make decisions, and regulate behaviour. They also support a sense of continuity and integrity – our personal truth. So, what's the downside?

Despite their advantages, this way of organizing information is prone to error. First, it heightens some data while downplaying others, more often focusing on the data that fit with the existing schema. This focus on consistency leads to a resistance to change, even in the face of conflicting evidence. Second, when novel information is allowed in, there's a tendency to 'conventionalize' it. That is, it's 'assimilated to fit cultural (and personal) norms, simplified and socially constructed in line with the way the group happens to be developing at the time'.[21] Third, in the absence of full information, our schemata contain best guesses or default values with which to plug the gaps. So, the way we process information and how we recall it are constructions (and reconstructions). This phenomenon is shown in research on eyewitness testimony in court cases. Recollections are affected by anxiety or stress, by leading questions, and by our tendency to fill in the gaps.[22] In many ways, we're all unreliable narrators of our lives who usually have absolute trust in our self-told stories.

Whenever we watch a film based on a true story, there's always a disclaimer that some of the details have been changed or added or that characters are composites. Anyone who knew about the life story of Freddie Mercury and then watched the biopic *Bohemian Rhapsody*[23] might have felt uncomfortable. I did. Key choices that Mercury made about his health and wellbeing, around the disclosure of his HIV diagnosis, were changed to fit a new narrative. In literature of *retroactive continuity* (or retcon, for short), it's the idea that 'history flows fundamentally from the future into the past, that the future is not basically a product of the past'.[24] This is something we do in the stories of our lives. Our memories do not replay recordings; they reconstruct narratives and distort anything that does not fit.

In the contemporary 'retelling' of mindfulness it has been conventionalized to serve the Western psyche as a stress-reduction technique. Stripped of its Buddhist ethical context and teachings, its secular version becomes a useful way to individualize stress rather than question why stress is so prevalent in organizations.[25] Professor of management and Buddhist teacher Ronald Purser, in his book *McMindfulness*,[26] offers a scathing assessment of mindfulness as capitalist spirituality – a new opium for the masses.[27] It is still slightly 'exotic', but ultimately something that challenges the Western mindset has been bent of shape to support the status quo. In its original context of Buddhist psychology mindfulness is more about gaining liberation from societal conditioning than adjustment to it.

Critical psychologist Ian Parker writes, 'Psychology as a discipline desperately tries to transcend specific local conditions in which it develops its theories and gathers together the "facts" supposed to support them, but it is always rooted in the particular conditions and biographies of those involved'.[28] How we define psychology depends on who we are, where we are, and the uses to which we put psychology.

Now, let's build on the working definition of the self from the introduction.

THE SELF AS A BRIDGE

The social self

We are social animals. We might even say we're 'hard-wired' for social interaction.[29] And our behaviour, thoughts, attitudes, and even our personality traits are shaped by our sense of belonging to a group.[30] For instance, you can't be shy on a desert island when it's just you and the coconuts for company. Overall, we don't cope well with social isolation,[31] and even when alone, we are affected by the implied presence of others.[32] And, as we have seen with the coronavirus protocols, the idea of two weeks social isolation is difficult for many people to process, both psychologically and pragmatically.[33]

When we focus on interconnectedness, social psychology and Buddhist psychology are similar. Although Buddhism goes a little further and holds that the independent self is a delusion and looks to transcend the 'I-other' distinction.[34] Social psychologist Roy Baumeister argues, 'solitary beings would hardly need or have selves'.[35] What would this mean for wellness? How could you be 'well in your self' if you didn't have one? But without a self, would you be in a state of bliss or a mindless zombie?

According to Baumeister, the self is as an interface or a bridge between our bodies and our social world. He argues, 'the self begins with the physical body, with acting and choosing as a unity, and as a point of reference distinct from others, and it acquires meaningful content by participating in the social system'.[36] Or put simply:

$$\text{Body} \rightarrow \leftarrow \text{Self} \rightarrow \leftarrow \text{Social System}$$

For Baumeister, selfhood helps us to function in the social and cultural systems which, at the same time, help to define our identity. These systems include family, school, clubs, gangs, local communities, hospitals, towns, corporations, cities, and countries. And to these, we can add the media, such as new sources, entertainment, and social media. We judge our wellness using the relatively stable sense of our self in line with standards of normality (in our social systems).[37] And the norms of different systems exert a different 'pull' on the self. We use stories to sustain a coherent whole and manage inconsistencies – as we become aware of them. Part of these stories includes how we value our selves – self-esteem – which often varies across settings.[38] In coaching, I get clients to track variations in their ratings of confidence, to pinpoint different narratives. By looking at a range of roles, interactions, and situations for the higher scores, they can see what they might 'borrow' to use for the lower-rated states.[39] It's a way of putting your best self forward.

The selfie effect

We can see the link between the self, the social, and the body in what plastic surgeons have dubbed 'the selfie effect'. Our social media passion for selfies[40] shows no sign of diminishing. We take, world-wide, about 93 million every day! But is this changing our view of ourselves? Well, in a survey of plastic surgeons, 42% reported they had patients who'd asked for rhinoplasty (nose jobs) to look better in selfies. It's because of wide-angle lenses on mobile phone cameras. When you take pictures too close to your face (30 cm), your nose will appear about 30% broader.[41] It's like looking at your reflection in the back of a spoon! But, rather than surgery, the answers lie in information and skills. Learn more about your camera, learn how to take better selfies,[42] or just look in the mirror. A selfie is like a distorted self-schema – it's all angles, tricks of the light, and digital filters, and 'going along with the crowd' which can cause us to question the evidence of our senses and question who we are.

'WHO AM I?'

20 Questions

In the classic parlour game '20 Questions', one person chooses an object that the other players must identify. To do this, they ask a series of closed questions – to be answered with 'yes', 'no', or maybe. This game has been an inspiration for many a quiz on the Internet (and self-help books). I took one such test, 'Can we guess who you are in only 20 questions?' I answered honestly. And it turns out I'm a 30-year-old, tanned, blonde woman with grey eyes. I have a great job but don't value it. But I do appreciate my partner. Although I am worried about having a third baby.[43] Uncanny! But does this type of vignette describe a person?

Sociologists Manford Kuhn and Thomas McPartland developed the *Twenty Statements Test* (TST)[44] to assess our assumptions and attitudes about the self. In the test, people are asked to write 20 answers to the question 'Who am I?' Each is in the form of a statement starting with 'I am'. These can be physical descriptions, interests, ambitions, values, social groups and roles, and self-evaluations.

To give an accurate sense of who you are, what are your 'I am' statements?

Wellbeing: the defining factors for you

The Office for National Statistics (ONS) in the UK asks four questions to tap into personal wellbeing,[45] rated on 11-point scales. The questions relate to life satisfaction, the feeling that the things we do in life are worthwhile, happiness, and anxiety. Respondents give an overall rating, on a scale from 0 to 10, in response to each question, where 0 is 'not at all' and 10 is 'completely'.

1 How satisfied are you with your life nowadays?
2 To what extent do you feel that the things you do in your life are worthwhile?
3 How happy did you feel yesterday?
4 How anxious did you feel yesterday?

How would you respond? Do these responses capture your sense of wellbeing? What factors influence your scores? What contributed to your happiness and anxiety? Do these single questions tap into anything meaningful? How can we be sure that everyone is responding to the same definition of happiness and anxiety? Are these simple questions an invitation to tell a story, or do they replace our stories?

In its analysis, the ONS considers the impact of a range of life factors that affect our wellbeing (or its limited analogue of wellbeing). These influences include our relationships, health, work status, leisure, where people live (local environment and community), and personal finances. As the circle widens circles, there's the state of the economy and governance (and particularly trust in governments). Finally, we have the effect of environmental issues, such as climate change. There is no strict order in which these might affect an individual's wellbeing. And all of the factors above are coloured by age, gender, and ethnicity.[46] What would you include? What about sexuality? What happens when your lived experience falls outside the discrete boxes on a form? All these factors intersect and interact. Our stories are greater than the sum of their parts and more nuanced than any statistical matrix can represent. For some of us, basic units of identity colour every aspect of lives. For others, the macro factors cast long shadows on the micro. And yet others just want to get through the day the best that they can.

What aspects gets in the way of your wellbeing or of you 'being you' and being well, and what confers the greatest wellbeing advantage?

A BRIEF HISTORY OF WAKING UP

Waking up above ground

In the vacuous world of motivational 'memes', the well-worn adage declares, 'If I wake up above ground, it's a good day'. More recently, the Japanese concept of *ikigai* has graced the self-help bookshelves. The word translates as the 'thing that you live for' or the 'reason you wake up in the morning'.[47] And then there's austerity ideology's appeal for team spirit after the financial crash of 2008 with its strapline 'we are all in this together'. In both cases, the assumption of sameness masks inequalities. Some of us were deeper in 'it' than others. And, some have fewer blessings to count. When we look at the World Health Organization's (WHO) definition of health from 1948, it is 'a state of complete physical, mental and social well-being'. Medical scholar and practitioner Dr David Misselbrook contends that WHO's definition is utopian and at odds with 'the struggles of real people in an imperfect world'.[48] Part of the 1948 Universal Declaration of Human Rights advances 'the right to a standard of living adequate for the health and well-being'. But what is 'adequate' and who gets to define it?[49]

Social scientist Professor Clare Bambra and colleagues assert that there's often an 'absence of mainstream debate about the ways in which the politics, power and ideology . . . influence people's health'.[50] They argue that heath is political 'because like any other resource or commodity under a free-market neo-liberal economic system, some social groups have more of it than others'. And it follows that this social inequality can only be addressed with political intervention.

A fairy tale about money

Austerity was not promoted as a political ideology but as a 'necessary evil'.[51] It has also been described as a 'fairy-tale about money' – albeit one without a 'magic money tree'.[52] But no matter how we 'spin the yarn', the cuts hurt the most vulnerable in society.[53] In parallel with spending cuts, in 2010, the UK government began to collect data on happiness and wellbeing. Part of the rationale was that a single economic measure (GDP) could not sum up the health of a nation,[54] and the new data would be used to shape policy.[55] But for some, it looked like an experiment in social engineering, with no happy endings. British Trade Unionist Len McClusky argued that the data would be used to claim that despite 'rising unemployment, home repossessions, longer NHS waiting lists and unaffordable education, the people of this country are happier'.[56]

In *The Spirit Level*, in 2009, two social epidemiologists, Professors Richard G. Wilkinson and Kate Pickett, compared the health indices of 23 countries and individual US states. Their results show that social problems, health, and wellbeing are worse in more unequal counties, whether rich or poor. Countries with narrower income gaps, such as Nordic countries and Japan, do best for their citizens. The most unequal countries do the worst, such as the US and the UK. They concluded that inequality erodes trust and increases anxiety and illness.[57] In 2011, a report by The Joseph Rowntree Foundation in the UK reviewed the research on income inequality, including Wilkinson and Pickett's findings. Its author, professor of social policy Karen Rowlingson, concluded that the literature shows general agreement about a correlation between income inequality and health/social problems.[58] A subsequent report for the foundation in 2015 concluded that most ethnic groups fared worse economically during the recession.[59] But several reports were not so measured in their assessment of austerity policies.

In 2017, a report by academics at University College London related spending cuts between 2010 and 2014 to about 45,000 more deaths compared with pre-2010 trends. The deaths were mainly of people over 60 in care homes. Another report in 2019 by the Institute for Public Policy Research (IPPR) showed a declining trend in preventable deaths between 1990 and 2012. But as public policy stalled because of austerity cuts, the rate of decline slowed. Had it kept pace with the earlier trend, the report estimated there would have been 130,000 fewer deaths between 2012 and 2017. Although in neither case can we infer cause and effect, the evidence for a link between austerity and avertible deaths is persuasive.[60] And, in 2018 in the UK, life expectancy progress 'stops for the first time'.[61]

The most damning assessment of the effects of austerity came in 2018, from the United Nations special rapporteur on extreme poverty and human rights, Professor Philip Alston. His report concluded that poverty in the UK is because of 'deliberate policy choices made when many other options were available'. Alston noted that standards of wellbeing had fallen markedly in a noticeably brief time, with over one fifth of the population living in poverty. He argues that successive governments continued, in a 'state of denial', to inflict the 'ideological project' of austerity 'largely unabated, despite the tragic social consequences'. Moreover, he described the Department for Work and Pensions (DWP) as a 'digital and sanitised version of the 19th Century workhouse, made infamous by Charles Dickens'.[62] Although we might argue that desperate times call for desperate measures, in a paper in 2009, professors of economics Robert Chernomas and Ian Hudson argue that the main aim of conservative economic policy is always 'designed to maximize the accumulation of profit while socializing the associated risks and costs'.[63] Bolstered by the myth of trickle-down economics, the gap between rich and poor widens. The response of the UK government to COVID-19 was a wave of spending to protect the economy. It is clear that public funding cuts have left the UK vulnerable and unprepared for the pandemic.[64] And yet the 'chief architect' of austerity, former Chancellor of the Exchequer, has warned that another period of 'belt tightening' will be needed to deal with the fiscal damage.[65]

But more than economic inequalities, another special rapporteur for the UN, Professor Tendayi Achiume, concluded that austerity measures had entrenched racism and stoked xenophobic sentiment in the UK. She argued, 'race, ethnicity, religion, gender and disability status all continued to determine the life chances and wellbeing of people in the UK in ways that were unacceptable and, in many cases, unlawful'.[66]

The great leveller?

During the pandemic, the 'great leveller' narrative appeared, and a BBC News presenter, Emily Maitlis, took issue with it.[67] In an introduction to a segment on the *Newsnight* programme exploring the economic impacts of COVID-19, she launched into a speech which divided opinion. Some praised it but others accused her or editorializing and damaging the impartiality of the broadcaster by not saying it was *her* opinion. She began, 'the language around COVID-19 has sometimes felt trite and misleading. You do not survive the illness through fortitude and strength of character . . . and the disease is not a great leveller'.

Maitlis argued that the consequences for rich and poor were very different, and those disproportionately affected, and most exposed to the virus, were the lower paid members of the workforce, such as hospital staff, care home workers, bus drivers, and retail staff. She concluded by saying, 'the World Trade Organisation warns the pandemic could provoke the deepest economic downturn of our lifetimes, we ask what kind of social settlement might need to be put in place to stop the inequality becoming even more stark'.

Early research into the first patients critically ill with COVID-19 in UK hospitals showed Black and Asian people were more likely to be severely affected by coronavirus than are White people. The Intensive Care National Audit and Research Centre found that 35% of nearly 2,000 patients were BAME people, almost triple the 13% proportion in the UK population as a whole. And the pattern is similar in the US.[68] One of the main explanations suggests an intersection with poverty. People in poorer or crowded living conditions cannot enjoy the luxury of social distancing.

In the UK the first ten doctors to die from COVID-19 were Black, Asian, and Minority Ethnic (BAME) people, prompting the head of the British Medical Association to urge the government to investigate why BAME people seem to be more vulnerable.[69] All this was amidst criticism of the failure to get personal protective equipment (PPE) to frontline healthcare staff. The BBC investigative programme reported that in effort to meet its target of one billion items of PPE, it counted single gloves, not pairs, to boost the figures.[70] But right-wing conspiracy-theory newspaper *The Daily Mail* asked, instead, 'how was the flagship BBC show infiltrated by the Left?'[71]

And then a step to the right . . .

To examine the political aftermath of financial crises, researchers analyzed more than 800 general elections. Their sample looked at 20 'advanced economies' between 1870 and 2014. And they found that in such times of uncertainty, the rhetoric of the right becomes more attractive to voters. On average, far-right parties increase their share of the vote by 30%.[72] This trend explains the Brexit result in the UK and the election of Donald Trump in the US, with a notable shift to isolationism, populism, and ethno-nationalism.[73] The Brexit referendum coincided with a spike in hate crimes, anti-migrant rhetoric, and racial, ethnic, and religious discrimination.[74] The response to the COVID-19 crisis has resulted in a suspension of civil liberties, such as in Hungary, with a removal of democratic norms.[75]

On being woke and the distress of privilege

The film *Pleasantville* is a visually stunning tale of political, social, and sexual awakening. In the film, two teenagers are transported to the black-and-white world of a 1950s TV show set in a midwestern US town.[76] Its themes help us to examine the ideas of 'wokeness', as well as the push-back against it. The term 'woke' is from African American Vernacular English (AAVE; meaning 'awake') and is used to mean being 'aware of and actively attentive to important facts and issues (especially issues of racial and social justice)'.[77] The call to 'stay woke' is credited to singer-songwriter Erykah Badu in her 2008 song 'Master Teacher'. As the popularity of 'woke' has grown, it has come to mean 'an informed, questioning, self-educating individual'.[78] But it has also become teenage slang or a social media hashtag to appear '#woke'. Politicians have criticized the casual use of 'woke'. LaKeshia Myers argues, 'not just be "woke" when it's convenient, but to stay woke even when it is most difficult or even dangerous. Being woke is more than a hashtag'.[79] And Barack Obama has challenged the idea that social media call-out culture has anything to do with social activism.[80]

Like the term 'political correctness', woke is used as a term of contempt by people on the right of the political spectrum who claim that 'woke' is a signifier of pretentiousness or virtue signalling. Or, some well-off, middle-class, White men who see any contests to privilege as racism against them.[81] And this development, dubbed 'the distress of the privileged', happens when 'people who benefitted from the old ways . . . see themselves as victims of change'. This idea is captured in the film *Pleasantville*, where the head of the household returns home from work to a new order with no wife, no children, and no welcome, summed up in his plaintive question 'where's my dinner?'[82] The director of the film, Gary Ross, describes the driving narrative as 'personal repression gives rise to larger political oppression'. He adds, 'when we're afraid of certain things in ourselves or we're afraid of change, we project those fears on to other things'.[83] In a zero-sum game, limited resource system, 'when you're accustomed to privilege, equality feels like oppression'.[84]

Perhaps the COVID-19 pandemic has ushered in better questions and conversations around privilege, inequalities, and wellbeing. In *Edelman's 2020 Trust Barometer*, 56% of people surveyed agreed that capitalism does more harm than good, and 78% agreed that elites are getting richer while regular people struggle to pay their bills.[85] Austerity ideology has meant that many people just have to take their chances,[86] and this has been magnified through the pandemic as many people in the gig economy have been abandoned.[87] There is a way beyond the 'us and them', one that doesn't involve 'attack and defend'. In his final 'Prime Minister's Questions', Labour leader Jeremy Corbyn called for bold, decisive, and collective action. He argued that the spread of COVID-19 had reminded us that 'no one is an island',[88] 'the least vulnerable in society makes us all vulnerable', and 'action to protect the most insecure and vulnerable is in the interests of public health as well as of social justice'. It's an argument reflected in the actions of the medical and academic communities. COVID-19 has shown us that our wellbeing is interdependent locally, nationally, and globally. [89]

Intersectionality revisited

Civil rights advocate and law professor Kimberlé Crenshaw coined the term intersectionality in 1989[90] to describe the way people's social identities, such as race, sex, gender, class, sexuality, and ability, overlap and intersect.[91] When asked to define the term 30 years later, Crenshaw says, 'These days, I start with what it's not, because there has been distortion. It's not identity politics on steroids. It is not a mechanism to turn white men into the new pariahs'. She explains, 'It's basically a lens, a prism, for seeing the way in which various forms of inequality often operate together and exacerbate each other'.[92] In Kate Bornstein's *My Gender Workbook*, she outlines a series of binaries: man/woman, Black/White, straight/gay, rich/poor, and so on.[93] One half of the pair is privileged over the other in that it confers a social advantage. Crenshaw states, 'Intersectionality is simply about how certain aspects of who you are will increase your access to the good things or your exposure to the bad things in life'.[94]

Sometimes, inequalities are not planned; they are a by-product of the scripts, schemata, and stereotypes we use to simplify the world. Consider the treatment of cardiovascular disease (CVD). Although more women than men die from cardiovascular disease, men are more likely to die younger. This influences the impression that it is a man's disease. So, models of treatment for CVD were developed using male patients, so women and men presenting with the same symptoms do not receive the same diagnosis and treatment. Men are more likely than are women to get further tests and preventative treatment. However, there is also an ethnicity bias, which, in the US, creates a double jeopardy for African American women whose CVD symptoms are most likely to be overlooked.[95] Crenshaw argues, 'being able to attend to not just unfair exclusion but also, frankly, unearned inclusion is part of the equality gambit. We've got to be open to looking at all of the ways our systems reproduce these inequalities, and that includes the privileges as well as the harms'. It's an awakening. And, as a way forward, 'self-interrogation is a good place to start. If you see inequality as a "them" problem or "unfortunate other" problem, that is a problem'.[96] The tragic killing of George Floyd on 25 May 2020 was the for catalyst for *Blacks Lives Matter* protests across the world. And the retort that 'all lives matter' is not an enlightened solution, it is a profound denial that speaks to the depths of the problem.

STORIES YOU LIVE BY

The stories of who we are and how we fit in are central to our wellbeing. We have a wide range of material on which we draw and many cognitive tricks and sleights of hand to make the information fit a coherent narrative. As clinical psychologist Stephen Briers argues, our stories 'exercise an inexorable pull over our actions, feelings and choices, rather like a magnetic field draws scattered iron filings into alignment with its own invisible lines of influence'. So as much as we organize our stories, they organize us. .

In *Twelve Steps to a Compassionate Life*, Karen Armstrong, comparative religion historian, outlines a programme for personal awakening. It includes many of the themes from this, and the previous chapter. And it's worth reading. It encourages us to read and learn more about compassion, to look at our own world, and to start with compassion towards our selves. It also invites to ask better questions and to try understand one another's narratives, even those of our enemies. Running throughout the book is the Golden Rule of 'Do not treat others as you would not like them to treat you' Or, in its positive form 'always treat others as you would be wish to be treated yourself'. And this leads to a most profound question: 'can we really count it as wellbeing if it comes at the expense of another?'

SUMMARY AND REFLECTION

In this chapter we:

- explored the idea that we are all storytelling psychologists, narrators and commentators trying to make sense of the world with our self-concept as a bridge.
- considered the role of cognition and schemata in organizing and distorting of the world.
- examined the idea of awakening to structural inequalities and how better questions will lead to better stories for all.

You have been invited to reflect a great deal already in this chapter, so I'll just ask, 'anything else?'

In the next chapter we explore the definition of normality and look at the main scourge of modern society – stress – and how to cope with it.

4

STRESS AND COPING

On being well in yourself

NO RETURN?

A graffito on a wall in Hong Kong during the coronavirus pandemic read, 'We can't return to normal because the normal we had was precisely the problem'.

Burnout due to overwork is a universal problem. But legislation, when it exists, more often applies to physical hazards, rather than psychological ones.[1] In 2019, a survey on work-related stress, published by the Health and Safety Executive, found there were 602,000 workers in the UK suffering from anxiety and depression. This led to 12.8 million working days lost, and the main causes cited – which are consistent over time – were workload, lack of support, and coping with change.[2] In the US, stress related to discrimination and poverty costs the US economy around $300 billion every year, in accidents, absenteeism, employee turnover, reduced productivity, and medical, legal, and insurance costs.[3]

When the World Health Organization (WHO) definition of health is 'complete physical, mental and social wellbeing', any deviation from perfection could be 'abnormal', and so needs to be fixed. But are any of us, ever, completely 'well in ourselves'?[4] Whatever the 'new normal' will look like, we can start by examining the old one. And part of that is asking, is stress always a bad thing?

In this chapter, we consider the question 'what is normal?' We explore the tension between survival and growth and consider differ models of defining and coping with stress.

WHAT IS NORMAL WELLBEING?

A matter of adjustment?

'Normal' is not so easy to define. And we don't question it, until our behaviour or that of others flouts unspoken rules. And yet, normality is another idea central to our wellbeing.

In his poem The Unknown Citizen, composed in 1939, W.H. Auden gives us a eulogy by a government bureaucrat to a model citizen.[5] The poem is in the form of a dystopian report gathered from the data sources of a hyper-vigilant, totalitarian state. The poem ends with the lines:

Was he free? Was he happy? The question is absurd:
Had anything been wrong, we should certainly have heard.

Throughout the poem, Auden touched on one of the main criteria for psychological normality. But underpinning it all, based on an unremarkable life, the man is judged a saint, based on his conformity, compliance, and predictability. And questions of freedom and happiness are meaningless. Psychiatrist Robert Lindner, in his criticisms of psychology and therapy, argue that they are tools of adjustment. But he doesn't see this as a good thing. He rails, 'Corralled in body an enervated in spirit by these delegated, elected, or self-appointed herdsmen of humanity, our society has been seized and help captive by the delusion that adjustment is the whole life, its ultimate good'.[6] For Linder, the 11th commandment is 'thou shalt adjust'. Are you normal? And how do you know? Let's consider several criteria we can use to answer those questions.

Normality – where do we draw the line?

There are several ways theories in psychology define normal. We can use statistics, societal norms, positive mental health, levels of personal distress, and maladaptiveness.

Statistical criterion

In psychology we assume that most human traits and characteristics confirm to the normal distribution. It's informally called a 'bell curve' because of its shape. In the absence of a diagram, it helps to compare it to 'Anne Elk's theory of Brontosauruses' from *Monty Python's Flying Circus*.[7] Her 'theory' states, 'All brontosauruses are thin at one end, much, much thicker in the middle, and then thin again at the far end'. And, so is the normal distribution. If we imagine a line running down the thickest part of the beast (or the peak of the bell curve), that's the average – the mean. This is the measure of central tendency for the range of scores. And in statistics we also need a measure of the spread of the scores. This is known as the standard deviation. One standard deviation either side the mean accounts for around 68%. And two standard deviations either side the mean accounts for 95%. This percentage we'd consider to be normal, given variations due to individual differences. That leaves the 2.5% at the extreme ends (the head and the tail). But the statistical criterion is neutral. It doesn't distinguish between atypical behaviour that is desirable versus undesirable – such as a creative genius versus the disturbed despot. Just because most people do it doesn't make it desirable or that they ought to do it.

Deviation from the norm

A deviation from 'the norm' implies a sense of oughtness – not behaving as one should. It's usually judged by external standards, such as society, culture, community, organization, or family. It is the need to meet certain expectations, or our perception of them.

Handwashing after we've been to the toilet has an oughtness, and we'd hope it would be the norm. During the COVID-19 crisis, we have been bombarded with reminders to do it and how to do it. From a statistical perspective, we'd expect a 95% compliance rate, but in a pre-pandemic survey of European habits, only two countries, Bosnia and Herzegovina (96%) and Moldova (94%), hit the mark.[8] At the bottom of the table of compliance, some countries were around the 50% mark (mentioning no names). But post-pandemic with 'the new normal' we might see fewer differences between countries. There are different norms within countries, between countries, and throughout history. During the pandemic lockdown, anxiety, stress, and boredom were the norm. And in some societies, sexism, racism, and homophobia were the norm, and probably still are to a less blatant degree. In some, they definitely are. And as we discussed in Chapter Three, when viewed through an intersectional lens, there are norms which we accept for others that we would not accept for ourselves.

Positive mental health

Social psychologist Marie Jahoda's 1958 book *Current Concepts of Positive Mental Health* is often relegated to a paragraph in introductory psychology textbooks. And the criticisms they offer are more to do with a misreading of the original book.[9] The idea behind the book was to gather the main strands of the various theories of positive mental health. She found six major categories of concepts from an extensive literature review.[10]

There are:

1 *Attitudes of the individual towards the self* – this included a realistic sense of selfhood in relation to goals and objectives. A sense of the real-self versus the ideal-self, and self-acceptance.
2 *Growth, development, or self-actualization* – to aspire to reach one's full potential. Interest and motivation to reach future goals.
3 *Integration of psychological functions* (incorporating 1 and 2) – a balance of conscious and unconscious forces, and to resist and cope with stress.

4 *Autonomy* – self-determination and independence. That is, overly ruled by environmental factors.

5 *Adequate perception of reality* – this means relative freedom from need-distortion, or in order words, not distorting information to how you want to see it. Also, having empathy and social sensitivity.

6 *Environmental mastery* – this includes achievement in some areas of life, adequate functioning in the world (focus on process – getting along). Examples of these include (a) the ability to love; (b) adequacy in love, work, interpersonal relations, and play; (c) efficiency in meeting situational requirements; (d) capacity for adaptation and adjustment; (e) efficiency in problem solving.

Of course, judging by these standards, none of us is normal – they are a collection of ideals. But we can see here a prototype for models of human flourishing in psychology.

In another of Jahoda's works on unemployment, she identified five factors vital to wellbeing that stem from being employed. We can apply these to the destabilizing effects of the lockdown during the COVID-19 pandemic. During this time many people experienced a loss of time structure, social contact, collective effort or purpose, social identity or status, and regular activity.[11] However, a main criticism of Jahoda's work is the Western-centrism. In her review of positive mental health, many of the concepts have meaning in individualistic societies, more so than in collectivist ones. And running throughout is the assumption that good mental health and wellbeing depend on adjustment and productivity.

As Jahoda's findings mentioned the self quite extensively, social psychologist Michael Argyle cites four major factors which influence the development of the self and how we evaluate it (our self-esteem):

1 The ways in which others (particularly significant others) react to us – whether people admire us, flatter us, seek out our company, listen attentively, agree with us, avoid us, neglect us, tell us things about ourselves that we don't want to hear.

2   How we think we compare to others – favourable versus unfavour-
    able comparisons.
3   Our social roles – some carry prestige and others carry a stigma.
    Some carry power and others are powerless.
4   The extent to which we identify with other people – roles aren't
    just 'out there'. They also become part of our personality, so that we
    identity with the positions we occupy, the roles we play, and the
    groups we belong to.

Personal distress

A key definition of normality is a subjective feeling of personal distress.
It might not be obvious to outsiders because we might keep such feelings hidden. Signs of personal distress can be both psychological and
physical. We might feel miserable, depressed, or agitated. Also, it might
disturb sleep patterns and appetite and manifest in aches and pains.

When I have initial consultations with potential clients, it is
common for them to ask whether coaching or counselling would
be the best way forward. I ask questions to find out the level of
personal distress. If their issues have a strong emotional part, then
I can refer them on to colleagues in counselling of psychotherapy.
Coaching is more about development goals.

Maladaptiveness

Sometimes people are judged 'abnormal' if their behaviour adversely
affects their own wellbeing or that of others – physically, psychologically, or both. The concept is of being a risk to one's own or others' wellbeing or safety. Through the various definitions of normality
there's a tension between 'fitting in' and 'just getting by' and the need
to thrive and excel.

SURVIVAL VERSUS GROWTH

If you've ever attended a training workshop, it's unlikely you have
avoided 'Maslow's Hierarchy of Needs'.[12] It's usually presented as a

pyramid, with 'self-actualization' at the peak – the idea that you can 'be the best possible version of you' – that's how self-help books describe it. And although it's overused, it offers a useful thread to link inequalities (from the earlier chapter) and stress.

- *Self-actualization*: realizing personal potential, self-fulfilment, seeking personal growth and peak experiences.
- *Aesthetic*: appreciation and search for beauty, balance, and form.
- *Cognitive*: knowledge and understanding, curiosity, exploration, need for meaning and predictability.
- *Esteem*: ego and status needs, and the need for recognition and to be valued.
- *Love and social belongingness*: family life, friendships, relationships, and intimacy.
- *Safety and security*: money, a job, health, and a safe environment.
- *Physiological*: food, water, sleep, and shelter – the basics to function/exist.

So as we move towards the top of the list we have growth needs, and as we move towards the bottom we have survival needs. We might call these basic needs the Four Fs (feeding, fighting, fleeing and 'copulating'). And the theory is that we need to satisfy the basic needs before we can satisfy the higher needs. Stress can occur at any level, depending on the pressures we face, the goals we have, and our resources to deal with them. We might experience frustration and conflicts, a disruption of bodily rhythms, life changes, daily hassles, or just the way we habitually deal with problems.

Psychiatrist Robert Lindner argues that our struggle to reach our full potential (or just survive) is a constant source of stress. According to him, we must conquer the 'triad of limitations' that forms our prison cell. 'One side is the medium by which we must live, the second is the equipment we have or can fashion with which to live, and the third is the fact of our mortality'.[13] It's bleak, but it resonates with the definition of wellbeing from the introduction – a state of balance between challenges and resources.[14] So, is wellbeing just the absence of stress?

WHAT IS STRESS?

How we conceive of stress determines how we respond and adapt to it, and how we cope with it. And we can advance three models of stress, each from a different angle:[15]

- *Stimulus* – stress is what happens to us.
- *Response* – stress is what happens inside us.
- *Transaction* – stress is what happens between us.

Stimulus – what causes stress?

In 1967, two psychiatrists, Thomas Holmes and Richard Rahe, created the *Social Readjustment Rating Scale* (SRRS). It consists of 43 life events, each scored to reflect the degree of adjustment it might need to get over them. These life events include the death of loved ones, divorce, personal injury, illness, losing one's job, trouble with the boss, and moving to a new house. It also covers marriage, retirement, gaining a new member of the family, and holidays. And it looks at changes in habits such as diet or sleep patterns. The scores of each event range from 11 to 100 and the total score is between 11 and 600. A score of more than 300 indicates a high risk of becoming ill.[16]

For Holmes and Rahe, stress in an independent variable that acts upon the individual. And although higher SRRS scores correlate with illness, the association is quite small. But there are several criticisms of the theory. It assumes that change is inherently stressful, and that life events demand the same level of adjustment for everyone. It also assumes a common threshold beyond which illness will result. Furthermore, it sees a person as a passive recipient of stress. Later advances in the theory include the role of the individual's interpretation of life events.[17] But, the model still ignores the effects of life experience, learning, environment, and personality. However, the SRRS is still useful as a basis for discussion in a therapeutic situation or for chats among family and friends.

Response – how we react to stress

In his best-selling book *The Stress of Life*, published in 1956, endo-crinologist Hans Selye outlines his general adaptation syndrome (GAS).[18] According to his theory, stress is a defensive mechanism and follows three stages: alarm, resistance, and exhaustion.

Gas: the three stages

Alarm: This refers to the first symptoms your body experiences in response to stress. The sympathetic nervous system activates these changes to prepare to combat or avoid the stressor (fight or flight).[19] Your heart rate increases, your adrenal gland releases cortisol (a stress hormone), glucose, and you get a boost of adrenaline, which increases energy.

Resistance: In this stage, if the stress is not removed the body begins to recover from the alarm reaction and to cope with the situation. Your body stays on higher alert and resists the stressor. If you over-come the stress or it ceases to be a problem, your body continues to repair itself. And your hormone levels, heart rate, and blood pres-sure return to pre-alarm states. In this stage you might experience irritability, frustration, and poor concentration. The parasympathetic nervous system restores returns physiological levels to normal. Also, this system causes the 'freeze' response in the body so that you feel unable to act or move.

Exhaustion: This stage is the result of chronic stress – struggling with stress for extended periods. It drains your physical, emotional, and mental resources. It can result in fatigue, disturbed eating patterns, anxiety, burnout, and depression. Physically, chronic stress impairs the immune system, making us less able to fight off attacks from bacteria and virus. It is also associated with asthma, colitis, and ulcers and is implicated in heart attacks and cancer. In fact, chronic stress has a negative effect on all bodily systems.[20]

It is neither possible nor desirable to remove every stressor from our lives. But if we spot the early warning signs for us, we can take steps to manage stress levels and lower our risk of the more serious conditions. Exercise, breathing exercises, laughing, and meditation can help your body to recover at the resistance stage and keep stress at a healthier level.[21]

What is healthy stress?

In *The Stress Concept: Past, Present and Future*, published in 1983, Selye distinguishes between bad stress, which he calls *distress*, and the good stuff: *eustress*. What we commonly call stress is distress, when we get a 'shut-down' of higher level thinking as we focus on basic survival needs (The Four Fs). In constrast, eustress is marked by focused attention and enhanced performance. Many of us need the threat of a deadline to get us started on a task.[22] This classification follows on from the Yerkes-Dodson law.[23] For complex, unfamiliar, or difficult tasks, we need moderate levels of stress for optimal performance. Without any stress we remain unmotivated, but when overwhelmed our performance declines.

Transaction – how do we cope with stress?

The transactional model sees stress arising between people and their environment. One problem with the SRRS is most of the 43 life events are not daily events. To explain stress as a more dynamic (and everyday) process, psychologists Richard Lazarus and Susan Folkman advanced the transactional theory of stress and coping. They define psychological stress as 'a particular relationship between the person and the environment that is appraised by the person as taxing or exceeding his or her resources and endangering his or her wellbeing'.[24] The appraisal is a process of categorizing any encounter in how it is likely to affect wellbeing.

The model applies two levels of appraisal, and then a choice of coping strategy:

- *First appraisal of the event* – Is it insignificant? Is it desirable or likely to benefit me? Or am I in trouble? Is it a threat, a challenge, or a loss?

(Here we might misperceive a trivial event as a threat.) Also, there's an appraisal of whether the challenge might become a benefit.

- *Second appraisal* – Do I have the resources for how to deal with the negative event to ensure a positive outcome? Can I cope with this situation? If not, a negative stress reaction occurs. Resources can be physical, social, psychological, or material. (Here we might not accurately assess our resources or lack confidence in our ability to cope.)
- *Coping strategy* – Based on the second appraisal we use either emotion-focused or control-focused strategies.

Emotion-focused coping

Emotion-focused coping involves trying to reduce the negative emotional responses associated with stress, such as sadness, fear, or frustration. If the stress is outside your control, then it might be your only option. Some of these strategies are quick fixes and can become habits, which also lead to stress. We might use food, distraction (watching TV), exercise, journaling (writing down thoughts), prayer, mindfulness, breathing techniques, or talking to someone (friends, therapist, coach). A therapeutic intervention can include a new cognitive appraisal of the stressful event. Of course, other emotion-focused strategies include alcohol, drugs, and gambling.[25] If you experience a bully in the workplace, start to keep a diary to deal with the emotion, which might later become evidence as part of a problem-solving strategy.

Control-focused coping

Control-focused strategies attempt to go to the source of the issue, such as problem solving, time management, new learning or training, and getting support, mentoring, or coaching.[26] This might also include getting more information to re-evaluate the problem. It might also include recourse to formal complaint procedures, or legal remedies. Other strategies include reading a book or controlling the amount of bad news you attend to.[27]

Another transactional model of stress involves taking control of the small stuff on a daily basis.

EVERYDAY HASSLES AND UPLIFTS

Psychologist Allen Kanner and colleagues[28] proposed a theory of stress based on the petty hassles we meet, such as losing keys, spilling drinks, or encounters with rude people. They composed a *Hassles Scale* of 117 items. They balanced this with an *Uplifts Scale* of 135 items, such as getting on well with people, receiving compliments, or just generally feeling good that day. In a study lasting over 12 months, the researchers found that hassles predicted negative psychological symptoms of stress, and hassles were a stronger predictor than that measured by the SRRS (major life events). One finding, useful for coaching, is that major life events, such as divorce, exert stress by several daily hassles. These including managing money, eating alone, or simply having to tell people about it.[29] And this everyday approach has two main benefits. First, it helps to break down major stressful events into manageable goals for control-focused coping, which, second, helps to tackle physical symptoms as they occur.

At the end of each day we do a mental balance sheet. If hassles outweigh the uplifts, we say we've had 'a bad day'. And for the opposite, we call it a good day. And the benefit of this approach is we can keep a check on the day to neutralize hassles and create our own uplifts.

And this idea of 'control what you can as you go' is a central theme in the idea of how some people manage change better than do others.

PSYCHOLOGICAL HARDINESS

Psychologists Suzanne Kobasa and Salvatore Maddi propose a combination of attitudes that creates a buffering effect against stress. Initially they studied male business executives to find out why some developed health problems while others remained healthy. And over the years the buffer effect has been shown in a large variety of groups including the military, firefighters, and university staff and students.

The three attitudes of hardiness have a moderating effect on stress by encouraging effective mental and behavioural coping, building and using social support, and practising self-care. Rather than a personality characteristic, it is more of an explanatory style – a series of attitudes (the three Cs) that shape our view of the world:[30]

- Commitment – 'a predisposition to be involved with people, things, and contexts rather than be detached, isolated, or alienated'.
- Control – 'struggling to have an influence on outcomes going on around oneself, rather than sinking into passivity and powerlessness'.
- Challenge – 'wanting to learn continually from experience positive or negative rather than trying to play it safe by avoiding uncertainties and potential threats'.

Maddi stresses the importance of adopting all three attitudes and not letting one dominate. Individuals 'high in hardiness' are more likely to put stressful life events into perspective and tend to perceive them as less of a threat and more of a challenge and as opportunities for personal development. Consequently, stressful events are less likely to impact negatively on a person's health.

In my coaching practice and confidence-building workshops, I use the three Cs to encourage clients to set small meaningful goals – to reach out and show curiosity about the world, to take stock of the small things that are already in their control, and to break down a larger problem into smaller challenges.

LIFE SKILLS/LEARNING SKILLS

In my professional practice I run a workshop, Learning Skills as Life Skills (and Vice Versa), which illustrates how we can bring together all aspects of psychology to improve wellbeing and enhance performance. It is a modified structure from my study skills book, Letters to a New Student.[31]

It offers a model to flourish in education as in life and draws on transactional theories of stress and control-focused coping. It's tempting to view formal education as learning and then everything else that happens afterwards as your 'real life'. However, it's a false dichotomy. We continue to learn throughout our lives, whether we want to or not. How we approach learning informs how we approach life and vice versa. I offer four interacting factors as a blueprint for lifelong learning: attitudes, wellbeing, cognition, and management. A change in one can have a knock-on effect in the others.

Attitudes

Attitudes are the cornerstone of how we make sense of the world. In coaching, I use the tenet 'the viewing influences the doing, and vice versa'. It's a key principle in confidence building that emphasizes the link between thoughts, feeling, and actions. How we view the world shapes what we do in the world.[32] The main strand in this factor is psychological hardiness – the three Cs.

Wellbeing

Wellbeing is a strong theme in the book, and is related to how we can reduce stress, improve mood, and boost cognition. The idea is to lay the foundations and give yourself a head start when studying. The wellbeing factor includes diet and hydration, exercise, sleep, and relaxation exercises and how they interact. When we feel stressed, these are often the first things we sacrifice. I'll outline, briefly, some of the intersections and how they support learning (and life in general).

- Diet. A healthy (no junk food) diet has a positive impact on gut bacteria (the microbiome), which helps us to absorb nutrients from food. As most of our serotonin ('the happy chemical') is made in the gut, a poor diet can inhibit it and lower mood and can be linked to anxiety. Although the research on hydration is mixed, some studies show that low hydration can impair cognition.[33]

- *Exercise*. We can boost cognition with just 20 minutes of aerobic activity, and this can also help improve your sleep. Exercise can also lift our mood, and short bursts of physical activity are useful in releasing stress and providing a break during long work periods.[34]
- *Sleep*. Unsatisfying sleep and disturbed routines have a negative knock-on effect for diet, and you'll be more drawn to junk food. Also, sleep loss can impair cognition and lower your mood.[35]
- *Relaxation*. Breathing exercises and meditation practice can help to reduce stress so that it stays in the 'eustress range' to improve performance.[36]

Cognition

The basis for efficient learning is to work with principles of psychology instead of working against them. This approach includes short but intense study periods and creating variety in study plans to appeal to all the senses, as well as leading your reading with questions to deepen understanding instead of using surface tactics like rote learning.[37] We look at a method of active reading in the next chapter when we consider how to make the most of a self-help book.

Management

Making the effort, actively, to manage moods, emotions, time, and resources will support the learning process. It's also about recognizing that boredom is a choice. We have the resources to tackle this negative attitude and create variety and contextual cues to improve cognition. Part of this is setting goals and using control-focused coping strategies rather than being ruled by our emotions, and part of managing learning and life is knowing when to ask for support and where to get it.[38]

MORE ON COPING WITH STRESS

Does mindfulness work?

Mindfulness is defined as 'the awareness that arises from paying atten-tion, on purpose, in the present moment, and non-judgmentally'.[39] It is often touted as the panacea for all ills. But is it? Well, the short answer is no. The evidence-based answer is more nuanced. First, the basic principle in psychology for treating anxiety disorders is that anxiety and relaxation cannot co-exist.[40] And, relaxation techniques for part of the core psychological skills for elite performance in sports psychology.[41] So, there is a basis on which to suppose that mindful-ness techniques have a beneficial effect.

A review of the research on the outcomes of mindfulness practices concludes that there is convincing evidence to show that they do help to lower stress, anxiety, and depression. And there are mixed findings on its effects to improve memory and attention. It has been effec-tive when combined with psychotherapy, such as mindfulness-based cognitive therapy (MBCT) for recurring depression. Although, it's no more effective than other forms of psychotherapy. However, in non-clinical settings, such as schools and the workplace, results are more mixed. It depends on how mindfulness is used, and how well the stud-ies are devised. There's also evidence of publication bias that favours positive results, which might exaggerate the effects of mindfulness.[42] So there is cause for some caution, but overall there is sound enough evidence to support the use of mindfulness as part of a holistic plan to deal with stress, as described earlier. But mindfulness on its own will not help to tackle the root of the problem, just our reactions. In many cases, that might be enough, but maybe we need to change the narra-tive. What if we challenged the Western appropriation of mindfulness and instead restore its own psychological roots. What if we used it in pursuit of a new normal to critique capitalism and consumerism?

Taking cures

Clinical psychologist Stephen Briers writes, 'people come into ther-apy . . . because they instinctively feel that the stories they have sought to live by are unravelling'.[43] Sometimes events can undermine our sense of self and challenge the narratives we hold to be true. Sometimes we entertain a number of self-stories that compete and conflict. Or we might find ourselves cast in a role we didn't chose or feel powerless to escape.[44] Left unchecked, chronic (long-term) stress can lead to anxiety and depression, and so in Briers's terms, therapy can help to 'forge a new narrative . . . one that reinterprets the past or opens up new possibilities for the future'.[45] But which 'talking cures' work best?

The equivalence paradox

When we look at the research comparing the outcomes from different types of therapy, one clear finding emerges. It's called the equivalence paradox. And it is best summed up by the verdict of the Dodo Bird in *Alice in Wonderland*: 'Everyone has one and all must have prizes'.[46] In other words, they all perform much the same. And these findings have been consistent since the 1930s. So no, cognitive-behavioural therapy (CBT) is not the answer to everything either, despite the hype.[47]

We can attribute a large part of the therapeutic effect to 'common factors', such as the relationship with the therapist (30%), and placebo, hope, and expectancy (15%). The specific techniques and models explain 15% of the treatment variance. And the largest factor, which accounts for 40%, is for the personal resources and life circumstances of the client.[48]

Finding help

The most important thing is to make sure you seek out a qualified therapist. Every country has accreditation bodies for psychotherapy, counselling, and coaching, and each has guidance on what questions to ask. However, many of the practical considerations are determined by how the sessions are funded. When funded by employers, health insurance, or a referral from your doctor, it tends to be for a fixed number of sessions. You are also unlikely to be given any choice in the type of intervention. However, research indicates that the optimal number of sessions is between four and ten. And surprisingly, the median number of therapy sessions is just one. We are not sure whether therapy didn't suit these clients, or whether one session was all it took to make a difference.[49] Finally we consider thoughts of a new normal. And this shift is not necessarily a new post-pandemic normal. That's likely to take time. It might just be something that's 'new to you'.

TOWARDS A NEW NORMAL

As the UK prepared to ease lockdown restrictions, writer Matt Haig tweeted, 'Yes lockdown poses its own mental health challenges. But can we please stop pretending our former world of long working hours, stressful commutes, hectic crowds, shopping centres, infinite choice, mass consumerism, air pollution and 24/7 everything was a mental health utopia'.[50] Haig has spoken and written about his own mental health. And his two self-help-type books seem quite appropriate for post-pandemic reflection: *Reasons to Stay Alive* and *Notes on a Nervous Planet*. Also, it's noteworthy that book sales massively increased during lockdown. And we know that reading lowers stress.[51] So, more books might be part of the new normal.

The COVID-19 pandemic has offered us an opportunity to pause, reflect, and take stock of attitudes, beliefs, behaviour, and routines. What insights do you have on your ability to adapt your thoughts, emotions, and behaviour as the situation demands? How has your understanding of yourself and others changed for relationships, communication, and social awareness? What small things can you control to make a difference? What power or influence do you have over the lives of others?[52] Of all the changes you had to make, what's worth hanging on to?

SUMMARY AND REFLECTION

In this chapter we:

- explored several criteria for normal in the context of wellbeing
- considered three ways in which to understand stress, that is, as a stimulus, as a response and as a transaction. mechanisms.
- looked at life skills as learning skills and how to cope with stress.

How has the information in this chapter affected your idea of 'normal wellbeing'? And what might a 'new normal' look like, for you?

In the next chapter we explore the self-help industry, including how to choose and use a self-book.

5

SELF-HELP AND WELLBEING

Ifs, nots, myths, and knots

RING OUT THE OLD; RING IN THE NEW

The first day of a brand-new year brims with symbolism and significance. Every January the obligatory 'New Year, New You' campaigns crowd the pages of lifestyle magazines pushing the next wave of self-help books. All urge us to transform our lives and unlock our 'authentic' selves. It's hard to put an exact figure on how much the self-help industry is worth. There's just so much of it.[1] There are 'infomercials',[2] self-help books, audiobooks and apps, weight loss programmes, motivational speakers, and personal coaching services. But the industry is most often valued around $10 billion as of 2016, in the US alone, with a forecast of about $13.2 billion by 2022.[3] Book sales slumped in the recession between 2007 and 2011[4] but picked up again with a boom in spiritual books in the 'mindfulness megatrend',[5] and more recently with a spike in sales of 'clean and tidy' books through the coronavirus lockdown.[6]

Many self-help books tread well-trodden ground; some state the obvious, some are pure invention, and some hold grains of truth. But among the deluge, gems can be found.[7] What we get out of these books depends on how we approach them. So, in keeping with sparkly metaphors popular in the genre, this chapter aims to help you 'grab the gold and pass on the pyrites'.[8] It is not a Dantean 'abandon hope all ye who enter here' diatribe.[9] It aims to inform and empower, with an eye on the evidence and the critical questions from Chapter 2.[10] We examine the origins of the self-help genre and some pop psychology myths that hinder more than help. And we conclude with practical pointers on how to pick a self-help book and make the most of it.

READ A BOOK – CHANGE YOUR LIFE?

Book therapy

Over the years, I've worked as an 'agony uncle' – an advice columnist in magazines and online.[11] Readers' letters, whether real or composites, often raise complex issues, but the word limit for replies is always tight. So, a key strategy is to address the broader issue in my response and suggest a self-help book to deal with the detail. The ones I recommend are evidence-based books by psychologists or psychotherapists.[12] They focus on a specific issue with advice for practical steps to resolve it. And generally, reading has been found to reduce stress, even if it's just a few minutes a day.[13] But there's a stronger precedent to use books in a therapeutic way.

Bibliotherapy is the use of novels, poetry, and storytelling for therapeutic purposes. It is defined as 'a process of dynamic interaction between the personality of the reader and literature . . . which may be utilized for personal assessment, adjustment, and growth'.[14] So books would be prescribed by a therapist as part of the healing process. And over time the concept has extended to include self-help books, with or without a therapist.[15]

What is self-help?

The dictionary definition of self-help is 'the action or process of doing things to improve yourself or to solve your problems without the help of others'. By extension, self-help books are a way of 'coping with one's personal or emotional problems without professional help'.[16] These books offer a cheap and accessible alternative to therapy, especially for less severe problems,[17] and the readers control when and where to read them. Also a book offers the opportunity to work on an issue in private.[18] But on the downside, a book offers a one-size-fits-all approach. There is no therapeutic relationship, which is a core factor in the healing process. So, a self-help book requires a more active role on the part of the readers. But might also selectively use parts of the book or misunderstand the author's aims and apply the advice in ways not intended.[19] Or they might not use any of it at all. A line from an online review of one of my books taught me a valuable lesson. It read, 'This is an average self-help book, as you do need to apply the advice within if you are to gain something'.[20] Sometimes people read books for comfort and not to be challenged. And as the self-industry thrives on repeat business, some readers become fans of an author or a concept.[21] Some might just enjoy being part of an 'in-group' of a new trend.[22]

Problems versus growth

Psychologist and happiness researcher Ad Bergsma identifies four categories of self-help book: *growth*, *relationships*, *coping*, and *identity*. He groups these into two themes: *problem-focused* and *growth-oriented*,[23] although some books cross over between categories and themes.

Problem-focused books include books on coping with stress, anxiety, depression, worrying, getting better sleep, dealing with burnout, how to manage emotions, dealing with life's obstacles, and mindfulness. This theme also includes relationship books both dealing with issues and improving communication skills.

Growth-oriented books include 'who am I?' personal growth titles, self-management, how to live a better life, making better choices, finding meaning in life, understanding yourself, finding your true self, and mindfulness.

Before assessing whether self-help books are effective, let's consider the readership.

Who reads this stuff? And who gets the most from it?

Women are more likely than men to have positive attitudes towards self-help books,[24] and female readers outnumber male readers by a ratio of more than two to one. Most are in the 20–49 age bracket, and about half (49%) have been in higher education.[25] There are some indications that readers have a wide range of interests, not just self-help.[26] These findings challenge the snobbish assumption that 'only stupid people read them', although some have noted, 'the more stupid the title, the better it sells'.[27] Also, philosopher Alain de Botton makes the case that many ancient philosophy books were self-help.[28]

Most self-help authors are men, for whom the gender split in readership is about 50:50. But for female authors, the readers are mostly women (87%). And in keeping with gender stereotypes, men are more likely to read books about careers while women are more likely to read books about relationships.[29] In traditional gender roles, males traits cluster around 'competence' and female traits around 'nurturance.[30] So, we might speculate that men view it as a sign of weakness to go into a bookshop for a self-help book,[31] unless it's a manly title by a man's man.

Psychologist Ad Bergsma reviews the outcomes of using self-help books and finds they are more effective when helping us learn new life skills, such as assertiveness, problem solving, and even tidiness. Although there's no support for the idea that a self-help book will transform your life, there is evidence that they can help to make more modest changes. One meta-analysis found that bibliotherapy was 'no less effective' than individual or group therapies.[32] Self-help books can also 'prevent part of the incidence of depression in high-risk groups'.[33] Several studies of people on waiting lists for therapy have shown positive consequences for people in a group receiving 'reading instructions' than those in a control group receiving none.[34] But it is crucial to take into account individual differences and the type of issues that affect them. Self-help treatments are more effective for milder cases of anxiety, depression, and insomnia, but not for smoking or severe alcohol issues.[35] Self-help has had the best success for people with higher motivation and who have more positive attitudes toward the treatments.[36]

None of these findings makes for great tabloid headings. Extra, extra, read all about it: self-help books work a bit, for some people, for some problems, some of the time! And although the studies are limited in design and sampling, they do suggest that self-help books have a supporting role to play in managing wellbeing. We just need to be sure we can trust the advice they offer.

THE SELF-HELP BLUEPRINT

Before writing a self-help book, I read a lot of them to see if I could work out the formula. And although I got a lot right, I made some 'rookie' errors. On reflection, I should have started at the beginning! Although there are many earlier self-improvement books, the archetype for the self-help genre is titled, not surprisingly, *Self-Help*, published in 1859.[37] Its author was a doctor, newspaper editor, and political reformer, the suitably named Samuel Smiles.[38] He was the great-great-grandfather of the explorer and motivational speaker Bear Grylls.

Self-Help was initially rejected by the publisher George Routledge, so the author pressed ahead and self-published it. It sold 20,000 copies in the first year. It was later picked up by another publisher, and by the author's death, in 1904, it had sold over a quarter of a million copies.[39] Among those inspired by it was Sakichi Toyoda, the founder of Toyota Industries, and a copy of the book is on display, under glass, at Toyoda's birthplace museum.[40]

Self-Help bears all the hallmarks of the genre and some warning signs to consider in any critical appraisal. It is full of anecdotes and inspiring potted biographies of 'illustrious men sprung from the ranks' and 'illustrious foreigners of humble origin'. The inference is 'they succeeded against the odds, so why can't you?' And, it asserts the way to success is through the virtues of labour, application, adopting better habits, self-reliance, strength of character, and self-education. Even today, the book has rich pickings for 'meme' creators: 'fortune favours the industrious', 'doing not saying', 'perseverance conquers all', and 'happiness and wellbeing are secured by our own conduct'. The author's follow-up books expanded on themes from the first, such as *Character*, and *Thrift*, then *Duty*, and *Life and Labour*. The content would sit well in any modern self-help book. Check out *Awaken the Giant Within* and *Unlimited Power* by Tony Robbins. They are not all 'Smiles', but they have their fair share.

No one could deny that Samuel Smiles was a remarkable man, but much of his work was 'of its time'. It's all very Dickensian. So, should it still be a blueprint for self-improvement today? Because the themes have a political agenda. And in his quest to push the myth of meritocracy,[41] Smiles popularized the idea of the 'undeserving poor'.[42] According to his view, the undeserving poor were those who didn't seem to want to work, and what they needed was a withdrawal of all state or charity support until they were forced to fend for themselves.[43] It's a 'no safety net, sink-or-swim' philosophy. So it is perhaps not surprising that, more than a century later, Conservative Prime Minister Margaret Thatcher wanted to give *Self-Help* as a gift to every schoolchild in Britain, and why a 'strivers' versus 'skivers' narrative was used to defend cuts in public services under austerity ideology after the financial crash of 2007–2008.[44]

Professor of disability and human development Lennard Davis criticizes the subtext of modern self-help authors. His words apply equally to Smiles's germinal tome. Davis argues that self-help writers work 'in the area of the ideological, the imagined, the narrativized . . . although a veneer of scientism permeates the work, there is also an underlying armature of moralizing'.[45]

So, I've learned, in my naivety, for my self-help book I didn't include enough 'moralizing', and I tried to pack everything I knew into one book, not string it out over four sequels.[46] I can live with that.

So, let's consider some of the more persistent tenets in self-help books.

POP PSYCHOLOGY MYTHS

Seize the day

During the COVID-19 pandemic, aside from fake news, the Internet proved a fertile breeding ground for inspirational 'memes', videos, blogposts, and social media posts. All of them imploring us to 'seize the day'. However well-meaning, they dripped with 'Smilean subtext'.[47] I read things like:[48]

- If you don't write your novel now, time is not the problem; you are.
- If you don't use this chance to take your business 'to the next level' you don't really want to be successful.
- If you can't commit to getting chiselled abdominals now, you don't want to be fit and healthy.

None of these statements recognizes the added demands of social distancing, whether practical, cognitive, or emotional. And they are all founded on antique myths. Clinical psychologist Dr Stephen Briers has also authored self-help books and admits to unwittingly repeating myths or simplifying evidence to support a point. Researching this book, I realize that I had been taken in by some of the myths too. In his book *Psychobabble*, Briers busts 23 self-help myths.[49] And, there are ten, at least, featured in Samuel Smile's *Self-Help* and repeated, uncritically, today. They are:

(i) let your goals power toward success; (ii) think positive and be a winner; (iii) you can learn to do anything you want; (iv) you'd better get yourself sorted (organized); (v) you are stronger than you know; (vi) you are a master of the universe; (vii) you are in control of your own life; (viii) make every second count; (ix) discover the real you; (x) we must all strive to be happy.

There are grains of truth in all these myths. However, they are often given as absolute truths with no consideration for individual differences, circumstances, and environment. And often, psychology shows that the exceptions are more compelling than the 'rules'. And, it's troubling enough there are so many myths, but doubly so when they are gilded with moralizing. This combination sets us up to fail and to feel guilty about it. In the final stages of writing this book, my working day started around 6:30am and ended at 10:00pm, and on a break I noticed this gem: 'In every day, there are 1,440 minutes. That means we have 1,440 daily opportunities to make a positive impact'.[50] And I thought, 'Thanks for that. Now I feel guilty for eating, sleeping, and sitting on the lavatory'. Thankfully, there are warning signs to alert us before we become too invested in 'guru-speak'.

Red flags/alarm bells

Four red flag statements that alert me that self-help guru is preaching pseudoscience. All these are false:

- Men and women are more different than we are alike.
- We only use 10% of our brains.
- Some people are 'right-brained' and some are 'left-brained'.
- In any communication, words only account for 7% of the message.

Gender differences

Consider the 'different planet' approach to relationships. Gender theorist Kate Bornstein describes such books as 'quick fix essentialism' which only work if we accept the first premise. Because when we ask questions, the arguments begin to unravel. Even basic ones such as 'Which women?' or 'Which men?' Intuitive sense-making is useful for forming hypotheses but flawed in finding out if they are correct.[51] Psychological evidence from multiple studies shows that differences between men and women are small. And even these tiny gaps are narrowing.[52]

Neurotrash

Cognitive neuroscientist Profession Gina Rippon coined the term *neurotrash* to describe pop psychology brain myths, including the notion of gendered brain differences.[53] No brain expert would use the terms 'right brain' or 'left brain'. They would more likely use 'hemispheric specialization'. So, if you see these simplistic categories, be suspicious. In fact, always be sceptical of any binary categories. The right-brain/left-brain theory is based on research of more than half a century of patients with brain damage.[54] Although we can pinpoint specialization of function in the brain, there is extensive interaction. But neuroscience has moved on since the 1960s, and more recent magnetic resonance imaging (MRI) does not support the idea of fixed lateralized brain types.[55] And, as for the 10% figure, it's hard to pinpoint where this started. One theory is that pioneering psychologist William James referred to 'underdeveloped potential' and a self-help guru decided to put a number on it. Also, early brain researchers admitted they didn't know what 90% of the brain did. And so, the myth was born. Over the years some attributed the statement to Albert Einstein, but no record of it exists.[56] This is a good place to mention neuro-linguistic programming (NLP). Although it has neuro in the title, it is not part of neuroscience but pseudoscience. At best, it takes three weeks to 'qualify'. And since the creation of NLP, there has been no research to support its 'extraordinary claims' in more than three decades.[57] There is also no proper regulation and standardization of training. In fact, one TV presenter, for an investigative report, managed to get his pet cat registered as an NLP 'Master'.[58] So, don't believe the hype.

The body language myth

I have included this by way of a confession. I am guilty of spreading this myth, but the last time was 2006. It's the famous '7%–38%–55% Rule'. The myth states that in any communication words only account for 7% of the message. The tone of voice accounts for 38% and body language and facial expressions for 55%. And it's true. These figures are from laboratory studies with female participants, although it was an artificial setting and a non-generalizable sample. So, we need to be cautious in our interpretation. Moreover, the research only refers to first impressions, or when words and non-verbal cues conflict. In these specific cases, we give more weight to the non-verbal content. But it does not apply to *all* forms of communication.[59]

None of these examples are likely to harm your wellbeing, but they show how the phrase 'research shows' or 'studies show' might be used to mislead. So, if a topic interests you in health and wellbeing, or learning, then examine the myths surrounding it and use the questions from Chapter Two to test the knowledge.

One aspect of pop psychology that deserves more scrutiny is 'the power of positive thinking'.

Toxic positivity

Sometimes it's not appropriate to 'turn that frown upside down' or tell people to 'smile, it might never happen' when it already has. Toxic positivity is defined as 'an ineffective and extreme overgeneralization of an optimistic, happy and positive state of mind in any given situation'.[60] During the COVID-19 pandemic, social media told us to keep smiling and that we'll all get through it. But fear, grief, and anger are appropriate emotions in a total disruption of normality and for such a high death toll. In the preceding chapter, one of the main criteria of positive mental health is an adequate perception of reality, empathy, and social sensitivity.[61] Unmitigated positivity is not positive mental health; it's denial. Author and political activist Barbara Ehrenreich in *Smile or Die* argues that the positive thinking movement has marginalized critical thinking.[62] Often it uses first-level intuitive thinking, confirmation bias, and cherry-picking that we explored in the preceding two chapters. And this 'pick and mix' approach can be dangerous. Essayist and investigative reporter Steve Salerno in *SHAM* argues that positive thinking can dissuade people away from proven medical treatments in favour of 'curing' themselves by the power of the will, with disastrous consequences.[63]

The 'GURU-ization' of self-help

The self-help industry becomes more intelligible once you stop seeing it as education or health information. It's infotainment, similar to the infomercial. In neither case is the primary aim to inform. Their aims are to entertain or to sell, respectively. And in some cases, to exploit for entertainment, such as scandal-based TV talk shows. It's all show business.

Adventures in infotainment

Hands up, I confess I have taken part in some PR-based research projects. But my criterion for taking part is that I need to be able to bring in evidence-based psychology. And that's why I turned down the Blue Monday campaign with its pre-written bogus formula.[64] They only wanted a male psychologist to put his name to it – because mathematics is a man's subject!

In the majority of media work, producers and directors are all very well-meaning, but I've lost count of times producers and journalists have asked me to say things that would 'make a better piece', irrespective of the evidence. I've been asked to 'speak more slowly', 'don't put so much psychology in it', and 'don't wear a jacket because it reminds the audience of bailiffs and debt collectors'. I've been told it's 'TV Gold' if you can make someone cry. And my own personal favourite was a proposal for a body language show that involved hidden cameras to film men at urinals. And when I protested that, aside from the ethical issues, if people know they are being filmed they will behave differently, the producer replied, 'Don't worry, they won't know they are being filmed'. As if this made it better!

As a public engagement psychologist, it's difficult to filter out the noise. I am often told by media producers and researcher that I'm being asked to comment on news stories because they have 'done their research'. But it's more likely they fiddled about for five minutes on the Internet, and once you are in their database, and have said yes once, the more likely you'll get asked again. When producers or journalists are under pressure they'll go to the convenient source, not necessarily the most appropriate. And the twin themes of entertainment and expediency explain why experts from the 'Oprah stable' like Dr Phil and Dr Oz were asked for their opinion about lifting the pandemic lockdown.

Neither are epidemiologists but they are experts at something, they are entertaining, and they said yes.[65] And even if they are speaking vaguely in their area, the commercial imperative might trump a factual one. A review of popular medical talk shows found potential conflicts of interest and that they 'often lack adequate information on specific benefits or the magnitude of the effects of these benefits'. Shockingly, half of the recommendations either have no evidence or are contradicted by the best available evidence.[66]

It is beyond the scope of this book to offer a complete dissection of the self-help infotainment industry, but two books I've cited by Barbara Ehrenreich and Steve Salerno are well worth a read.[67] The mass media are indispensable for drawing out attention to ideas, new and old, and new products and trends in self-care and wellbeing. However, we always need to bear in mind that they are often unreliable narrators.

DOING IT BY THE (SELF-HELP) BOOK

Self-help double binds

Just like the impossible objects of artist M.C. Escher,[68] pop psychology creates Escher-like impossible objectives. In self-help books there is often a tension between high self-esteem and unrealistic 'change your life' goals, or multiple goals, or mixed messages. These can set up double binds[69] or what psychiatrist R.D. Laing calls 'impossible knots'.[70] For instance, how do we respond to the societal maxims of 'look before you leap' and 'they that hesitate are lost'? Or, 'you are the Master of your own destiny' and 'trust in the Universe'? And the same applies when too many goals conflict.[71]

Pop psychology has no overarching paradigm. It can be an 'anything goes' model, where theories and ideas are cherry-picked to support a first premise that might not be true.[72] Pop psychology books might be presented as theories, but theories need to be tested.[73] Otherwise you're just being drafted into someone else's wishful thinking.

The anti-self-help book

Steve Salerno's SHAM inspired a new trend in self-books. What began as a handful of books warning of the perils has now become a new shelf in the pop psychology section – the anti-self-help book. Just what we need – books that advise us not to read advice books. But unless you're loitering in book shops reading them for free, someone is making money from them. And the same rules of critical analysis apply. Who is the author? What are their credentials? What are their qualifications, accreditations, and professional memberships? And is there any substance to the approach? Among the new wave are books with expletives in the titles such as John Parkin's F**k It: The Ultimate Spiritual Way. And it's a fun idea. But as amusing as it is, does it really need a 777-page book, let alone several books to tell you that saying 'f**k it' is a spiritual act? And does it need a residential retreat in some sunny clime to immerse yourself in the therapeutic power of 'f**k it'?[74] Because if you don't f**k it after the first page you probably never will.

So now, with the main caveats covered, if you are in the market for a self-help book, let's explore how best to find one that works for you.

How to get the most from a self-book

In this last section, we draw together themes from the book so far to form a basis to choose and use a self-help book.[75] But before we consider the pointers, in theory, can a self-help book really help? Well if we go back to the discussion in the preceding chapter on therapeutic outcomes, it provides some 'ifs'. From the preceding chapter on outcome research, a book can offer hope and have an expectancy effect. The missing factor is the relationship, which is not likely to be as strong between a reader and an author. That's why celebrity self-help books do well. There's a sense of knowing the author. And if you a chose a book where the author's voice comes through in the writing, this can help to create a sense of a relationship. But overall, the success of a self-help book lies in how you read it and what you do with the information.

Chose a book like you'd choose a therapist

If you choose a self-help book like you'd choose a coach or a therapist, everything begins to fall into place.[76] If you check the author biography and it states they talk to angels, are the reincarnation of Nefertiti, and were raised by wolves, chances are it's not an evidence-based approach. All the critical questions proposed in Chapter 2 will help you to decide if the author is an expert at all, and an expert you can trust. And look out for the self-help myths covered earlier.

Websites such as *Reading Well*[77] in the UK works with libraries to recommend booklists chosen by experts and by people living with conditions covered in the lists, and their relatives and carers.

Does it speak to you?

Once you have checked the book's credibility, move on to the tone. Do you like the style and layout of the book? Does the way the book is written 'speak to you'? Does the book impose a story on you, or does it help you to retell your story? Is the book likely to motivate you?

Actively engage with the material

A common mistake made in study skills is an over-reliance on passive techniques, learning by rote, and trying to memorize lecture notes.[78] However, we retain information better the more we do with it at the input stage. And we can borrow this idea from study skills and use an active reading technique for self-help books. It helps to use a journal to capture your thoughts, the outcomes of any exercises, and your reflections. I have adapted the academic and the SQ3R technique for use with a self-help book. This revised version stands for survey, question, read, react, review.[79]

- **S**urvey – flick through the book to get a feel of the structure and layout. This stage incorporates some of the insights from 'Does it speak to you?' mentioned earlier.
- **Q**uestion – from the start write questions in your journal, for the book as whole, and then for each chapter. What questions do you want the book, and each chapter, to answer? This tactic helps to create a context for processing the information.
- **R**ead – as you start reading, keep your questions in mind, and write down thoughts, questions, and reflections as you go.
- **R**eact – is another way of saying 'if the book has exercises, suspend your belief and try them out'. Attitude change involves thoughts, feelings, and actions. And often the easiest way to create some fresh insights is to take action, and then reflect.
- **R**eview – at the end of reach chapter, take a few moments to consider the information before moving on to the next chapter.

Shared experience

The *Reading Well* website has a function for finding reading friends. So, to enhance the experience further you could work through a book with a friend or set up a reading group – like group bibliotherapy.[80]

And that's how you make the most of a self-help book and improve your chances of having a positive experience. A book probably won't change your life. But rather than being a 'punter' in a commercial process, you create your own process in a way that just might help your self.

SUMMARY AND REFLECTION

In this chapter we:[81]

- examined the 'self-help trade' and whether it harms more than it helps
- narrowed the applications of self-help materials to areas where it is likely to be more effective

- explored the origins of the self-help book genre, exploded some pop-psychology myths, and outlined a plan to select a self-help book and make the most of it.

How has the information affected your approach to wellbeing? And what ideas do you have for further investigation?

In the next chapter we examine the contributions that positive psychology has made to our understanding on wellbeing.

6

HAPPINESS, MEANING, AND THE GOOD LIFE
The structure of wellbeing

ON THE BRIGHT SIDE

In 1998 'positive' was the watchword in psychology. It was the year Professor Martin Seligman chose positive psychology as the theme for his term as president of the American Psychological Association (APA). And so, a new domain of psychology was born: 'the scientific study of what makes life most worth living'.[1] Positive psychology's aim is to '[bring] the same attention to positive emotions (happiness, pleasure, well-being) that clinical psychology has always paid to the negative ones (depression, anger, resentment)'.[2]

Since its start, positive psychology has grown exponentially with academic programmes across the world, featured in major publications such as *Time* and *Newsweek*, and attracted millions in research funding. The International Positive Psychology Association now boasts thousands of members in 70 countries.[3] And Seligman even had the ear of the UK government when it decided to collect data on the nation's wellbeing.[4]

In this chapter, we explore the main topics of interest for positive psychology, including subjective wellbeing, the search for meaning in life, and how we can all flourish. It also examines the origins and some limitations of positive psychology and provides a suggestion for its development.

WHAT IS POSITIVE PSYCHOLOGY?

Many years ago, in a talk as part of an interview process, the moment I said, 'positive psychology', two people in the room rolled their eyes like slot machines. I suspect they had conflated positive psychology with the concept 'positive thinking' (from Chapter 5).[5]

The mission

In 2000, Seligman and Mihaly Csikszentmihalyi[6] laid out their vision for the future of psychology in their paper *Positive Psychology: An Introduction*. Its emphasis was on a 'science of positive subjective experiences, positive individual traits, and positive instructions'. To be more specific, the subject material of their vision for psychology is 'valued subjective experiences' such as 'wellbeing, contentment, satisfaction (in the past), hope and optimism (for the future), and flow and happiness (in the present)'.[7] It's about how people flourish. So, a fuller definition of positive psychology is 'the scientific study of positive human functioning and flourishing on multiple levels that include the biological, personal, relational, institutional, cultural, and global dimensions of life'.[8] The paper has the tone of a manifesto, and some critics argue that it exaggerates the negative aspects of past psychology and underplays its positive aims and impact. So, when Seligman and Csikszentmihalyi criticize psychology's 'almost exclusive attention to pathology',[9] we must ask, 'Which psychology?' Because it only makes sense if it refers to clinical psychology and psychotherapy. Not all psychology. And it also downplays humanistic psychology on which their new field is based. The term positive psychology was coined in 1954 by Abraham Maslow in his book *Motivation and Personality*.[10] If you have been to a training seminar on 'how to reach your potential', you will have heard of Maslow's Hierarchy of Needs – with *self-actualization* at the top of the pyramid (and in the last version, the peak became *self-transcendence*). And going way back to *The Principles of Psychology* by William James in 1890, subjective experiences were there from the start.[11] But these criticisms and observations help to widen the scope of the psychology of wellbeing and provide suggestions for ways forward.

Happy lives – different angles

You're standing in front of two doors, and both promise a happy life and positive wellbeing. One door is marked 'Pleasure' and the other 'Meaning'. Which would you choose?

These doors stand for two main themes in wellbeing research. Pleasure (or happiness) is known as *hedonia*, and meaningfulness is *eudaimonia*. Or at least there used to be two doors. But Seligman, in his TED Talk titled 'The New Era of Positive Psychology', describes three types of happy lives, *the pleasant life, the good life, and the meaningful life*. But they don't map on to traditional meanings. The pleasant life is hedonia, confusingly his good life is eudaimonia, and his meaningful life seems to be mixture of the two. And furthermore, he's quite disparaging about hedonic wellbeing, referring to it as 'the whipped cream and the cherry'.[12] So, rather than a coherent 'fourth wave' of psychology, as promised, there still 'seems' to be a 'jockeying' for position – 'my wellbeing is bigger than yours'.

My solution is to present the concepts of *subjective wellbeing, flow*, and *flourishing*, and comment on how they fit into the hedonic–eudaimonic scheme.

SUBJECTIVE WELLBEING

Subjective wellbeing (SWB) is another way of saying hedonic wellbeing. Psychologist Ed Diener is the main authority, and work on SWB started in the 1980s. It has earned him the nickname 'Dr Happiness'. His three-way model of SWB tackles the question from Chapter 3, 'How are you in yourself?' The three distinct but related components are frequent positive feelings, infrequent negative feelings, and evaluations of such as life satisfaction – how well you think your life is going.[13] The first two components taken together are called *affective balance* – that is, weighing up emotions, moods, and feelings. And the third part, the cognitive evaluation, can be a global judgement of your life or specific areas of life. SWB is typically measured with various psychometric questionnaires.[14] Using this method, wellbeing is assessed in a series of quantitative test scores.

Research shows that improvements in the environment temporarily boost SWB, but people soon get used to the beneficial changes and SWB returns to the baseline. But when people seek to increase SWB by their actions, the effects endure longer.

The next concept is all about action.

FINDING FLOW

We talk about 'getting in the groove' or 'being in the zone'. For psychologist Professor Mihaly Csikszentmihalyi, this concept is known as *flow*. It's a psychological state of 'being completely involved in an activity for its own sake. The ego falls away. Time flies. Every action, movement, and thought follows inevitably from the previous one. . . . Your whole being is involved, and you're using your skills to the utmost'.[15] You might experience flow when you play a musical instrument, are engrossed in a hobby, or when playing sport.

Flow is that experience of losing sense of yourself and time. And for Csikszentmihalyi, the more time we spend in flow, the happier we are. But it just doesn't happen on its own; we must work at it. Flow, according to him, is prepared for, cultivated, and defended. In his book *Finding Flow*, he explains the concept in terms of two dimensions: challenge and skill.[16] And for each of the dimensions, there are three degrees: low, moderate, and high. The various combinations of these dimensions and degrees describe eight psychological states. The undesirable ones are anxiety, worry, apathy, and boredom. The desirable states are arousal, relaxation, control, and flow. There is no state specified for moderate challenge and skill, unless you can think of one. And arousal, in this context, is better understood as 'alert and engaged'.

	Low Skill	Moderate Skill	High Skill
High Challenge	Anxiety	Arousal	Flow
Moderate Challenge	Worry	–	Control
Low Challenge	Apathy	Boredom	Relaxation

Table 6.1. Eight Psychological States (Challenge by Skill).

With my clients for academic coaching, 'apathy and boredom' are the two most frequent complaints about studying. But most often, they are choices. And using the concept of flow, we can use a higher-level skill (which is more work) or set a higher challenge,[17] which will change the state into arousal or control. To process the information cognitively to a deeper level, we must do more with it, which then makes it more interesting.

We can use the concept of flow for any type of goal setting. In coaching I start by getting clients to set small goals aligned with their skills and strengths (using the states of relaxation and control). As Csikszentmihalyi guides, 'You need clear goals that fit into a hierarchy, with little goals that build toward more meaningful, higher-level goals'.[18] Also, you'll notice the similarities and parallels with the theories discussed in Chapter 4, such as eustress, psychological hardiness (commitment, challenge, and control), and the hassles and uplifts theory of stress. Used together, all these form a compelling strategy for coaching to create order, build motivation, and enhance wellbeing. But what's most striking is within Western psychology, flow has the hallmarks of Buddhist psychology. Flow is a Zen-like state about being mindful, in the moment, and enhancing wellbeing by losing sense of one's self.

FLOURISHING AND THE STRUCTURE OF WELLBEING

In 2011, Martin Seligman, in his new book Flourish: A Visionary New Understanding of Happiness and Well-Being, sought to shift the argument away from happiness to a multi-dimensional approach.[19] Flourishing describes an optimal range of human functioning, 'a state where people experience positive emotions, positive psychological functioning and positive social functioning, most of the time'. Its opposite is *languishing*, one where life feels empty and uninspired.[20] There are many competing models of flourishing within positive psychology, but they cover much the same, just with differing emphasis.

Models of flourishing

For his model, Seligman uses the mnemonic PERMA. This stands for:

- **P**ositive emotion – which is another way of saying subjective well-being (hedonia)-feeling good.
- **E**ngagement – which is another term for flow.
- **R**elationships – this refers to positive social connections, friends, family, and intimacy.
- **M**eaning – which is close to eudaimonia, that is, having a purpose in life and belonging to something greater than oneself.
- **A**chievement – this refers to the concept of self-actualization. It's about having goals (and reaching them).

Seligman's was not the first exploration of the topic. In 2002, psychologist Corey Keys and Jonathan Haidt gathered together several scholars for their volume *Flourishing: Positive Psychology and the Life Well-Lived*.[21] The main themes include rising to life's challenges; engagement and relating; fulfilment in creativity and productivity; and looking beyond oneself and looking ahead.

Earlier still, in the 1980s a six-factor model of psychological wellbeing was proposed and evaluated. Although not called flourishing, it is a prototype. The factors include self-acceptance, personal growth, purpose in life, environmental mastery, autonomy, and positive relations with others. The only thing missing is a measure of subjective wellbeing. You will notice that Ryff's model is based on Marie Jahoda's positive mental health criteria (Chapter 4).[22]

The next example is not, strictly speaking, as a model from positive psychology, but it is a model of flourishing.

Ikigai

The Japanese concept of ikigai has been Westernized to tie one's life purpose to a paid vocation (career). Used this way it's just an elaborate work-life balance model. And this rush to fit the concept to Western schemata means crucial detail has been lost in translation. Tim Tamashiro, jazz singer, broadcaster, and speaker in his TED Talk 'How to Ikigai',[23] describes ikigai as a treasure map with four directions. It is expressed as a Venn diagram of overlapping circles with ikigai at its centre. These are (i) do what you love; (ii) do what you're good at; (iii) do what the world needs; and (iv) do what you can be rewarded for. In a survey of Japanese people in 2010, less than a third (31%) work as their ikigai.[24]And this version recaptures some of sense that we can 'ikigai' (as a verb) in any aspect of our lives.[25]

In his research, clinical psychologist Akihiro Hasegawa discovered that Japanese people believe that the sum of small joys in everyday life results in more fulfilling life as a whole. This aligns with the everyday hassles and uplifts theory of stress we discussed in Chapter 4. Neuroscientist Ken Mogi simplifies the Venn diagram approach to five key pillars to ikigai: (i) starting small (goals); (ii) releasing (accepting) yourself; (iii) harmony and sustainability (socially and environmentally); (iv) the joy of little things; and (v) being in the here and now (mindfulness).

In the 1960s, psychiatrist Mieko Kamiya identified seven ikigai needs: (i) the need for a fulfilling existence; (ii) the need for change and growth; (iii) the need for future perspectives; (iv) the need for receiving responses; (v) the need for freedom; (vi) the need for self-actualization; and (vii) and the need for significance and value.[26] And Kamiya maintains that it can harmful to the individual to try to force one's ikigai (meaning of life) to match what one does for a living. And it doesn't matter if we don't meet our goals, it's enough to be on the path to meet them. It's like Maslow's idea of 'growth motivation' (as opposed to mere survival) in humanistic psychology.[27] And in this scheme, ikigai is what allows you to look forward to the future even if you're miserable right now.[28] Just from this brief review of Positive Psychology, we can see that there is potential to consider ideas outside the Western mindset. But, newer developments suggest a narrower view.

FURTHER DEVELOPMENTS IN WELLBEING RESEARCH

In a plenary discussion titled 'The Future of Positive Psychology' at the Sixth International Positive Psychology Summit, Martin Seligman suggested the way forward was a plural theory, taking in anthropology, political science, and economics. This approach would be a shift to 'positive social science'. According to writer and political activist Barbara Ehrenreich, the suggestion was not well received by the several hundred positive psychologists, graduates, and coaches in attendance. But some of the recent suggestions for future research go further with speculations about the use of technology looking less and less like psychology. Suggested avenues of research include big data machine learning predictive algorithms, psychopharmacology, non-invasive brain stimulation, and virtual reality.[29] Seligman has started a big data project called the *World Well-Being Project*. Its website describes it as 'a pioneering scientific techniques for measuring psychological well-being and physical health based on the analysis of language in social media'.[30] It's a collaboration between psychologists, statisticians, and computer scientists aimed at 'exploring the potential for our unobtrusive well-being measures to supplement – and in part replace – expensive survey methods'. All of this seems far removed from happiness questionnaires and from everyday life.

CRITICISMS OF POSITIVE PSYCHOLOGY

A wave of optimism

A frequent criticism of positive psychology is that it has been a little too optimistic in its interpretation of the research findings. And in one instance, mathematical modelling of positive emotions was debunked by an amateur mathematician.[31] There's also the push to find a potential genetic effect on wellbeing and happiness. The nature versus nurture debate is familiar to every psychology student. The case for nature rests on evidence from twin studies. These studies compare identical (monozygotic) twins with non-identical (dizygotic) twins. The monozygotic (one-egg) twins share 100% of the genetic material, while the dizygotic (two-egg) twins share only 50% of the material. The theory suggests that this separates the genes from the upbringing and environment. However, in the 1960s it was conceded that identical twins experience more similar environments than do non-identical twins. And yet, as clinical psychologist Jay Joseph argues, 'instead of relegating the twin method to a place alongside other discarded pseudosciences', researchers continue to try to refine it. We cannot 'disentangle the potential roles of genetic and environmental influences' on behavioural traits.[32]

Not the whole story

What positive psychology misses is as telling as what it includes. It does not address how we make sense of negative emotions and experiences and use them for positive outcomes. And most importantly, it does not question power, privilege, and social hierarchy. How do they impact on the pursuit of the good life? Who is excluded and who gets to 'flourish' at the expense of others?[33] From this perspective, there's the same 'who dares wins' ideology of Samuel Smiles's *self-Help*. And from the proposals for new technologies, positive psychology at the 'cutting edge' seems to have lost sight of its founding ideas of helping people. Instead, in this *Brave New World*,[34] it is edging towards an array of things that can be done to people. And the warnings from Stanislav Andreski's 1972 book *Social Science as Sorcery* no longer seem that extreme. He writes of being caught up in 'fashionable but irrelevant paraphernalia' of simulation models and algebraic symbols. He also cautions of a sinister alliance between '"academic callboys" who knowingly or unknowingly, serve the interests of the wielders of power and the "Foundation moguls" by putting pseudo-scientific gloss on the crude realities of power and giving their blessing to the status quo'.[35] His is one of many radical books in the 1970s challenging psychology and education. It's time to reboot and reread and decide what the average person needs and wants from the psychology of wellbeing, and not just follow where the funding leads. Do we trust a psychology that increasingly takes away the opportunity to tell our own stories?

WAYS FORWARD

Positive psychology began by presenting itself as a fourth wave. It was an evolution from psychoanalysis, behaviourism, and humanistic psychology. That path marks a shift from unconscious drives to behavioural conditioning, to understanding our lived experiences, to flourishing. But psychologist Kirk Schneider makes the case that positive psychology is a branch of humanistic psychology, and from the brief review in this book, that case holds.[36]

By embracing its roots, positive psychology opens up to a broader range of research methods. For an area of psychology that champions the meaningful life, there is little room for meaning in the methods it employs. Humanistic psychology is not averse to using personality measures and psychometrics but meaningfulness to the individual is always at the centre.[37] A matrix of numbers from a combination of factors might be an analogue of wellbeing but it needs a back story. Psychotherapist Dana Becker and psychologist Jeanne Marecek in their analysis of the history of positive psychology argue that there are comparisons with 19th-century popular mind cures with their emphasis on individual and adjustment. And they say that what is needed is a more radical approach that focuses 'beyond the individual in isolation, a perspective that takes in the totality of the social environment and an ethical stance that values social engagement and activism'.[38] Controversial firebrand feminist Germaine Greer argues that gender equality is rather a conservative goal,[39] because it assumes that what you want to be equal with is *worth* being equal with. And this principle applies to the goal of adjustment. Is that a worthy goal? What if adjustment is part of the problem in our quest for happiness, meaning, and wellbeing? For Greer, the goal should be liberation. She argues, 'Liberation struggles are not about assimilation but about asserting difference, endowing the difference with dignity and prestige and insisting on it as a condition of self-definition and self-determination'.[40]

SUMMARY AND REFLECTION

In this chapter we:

- considered the contribution of Positive psychology to our understanding of wellbeing.
- looked at through the concepts of subjective wellbeing, flow and flourishing, and considered some overlaps with Buddhist/Zen psychology.
- considered further developments, criticisms of Positive psychology and potential ways forward.

What factors would you include in your model of flourishing? And where do you think the domain of Positive psychology should focus its attention in the pursuit of a greater understanding of wellbeing?

In the final chapter we draw together the themes of the book with some concluding thoughts, reflections, and a story to structure your wellbeing goals.

7

SOME CONCLUDING THOUGHTS . . .

Stories, questions, and reflections on being well and getting better

TO BE CONTINUED. . .

In the introduction, I questioned whether psychology had anything to say about wellbeing. And now I'm beginning to think it has too much to say for itself. So much of what I read and wrote didn't make the final edit. Although I covered most of the material from the original proposal there are things I didn't expect to find or include. For instance, I did not expect to find so many connections with Buddhist psychology in how I practice coaching. This book has been a journey for me, and there have been numerous times when I've complained that writing a book on wellbeing should carry a government health warning. And when I've protested 'never again'.[1] Hopefully it hasn't been such a painful read. Perhaps there are things you expected the book to cover, but didn't. These are continuation paths for your reading, writing and research into wellbeing. It's where you take up where I left off.

While considering how I might escape the 'traditional' conclusion, I found a transcript online of a lecture from 2010 by Martin Seligman,[2] *Flourish: Positive Psychology and Positive Interventions*. Here was the face of positive psychology finishing with a tale from Friedrich Nietzsche's *Thus Spoke*

Zarathustra: A Book for All and None. Wellbeing is not the first word that springs to mind when you think of Nietzsche.[3] And yet, somehow, here we are.

THE CAMEL, THE LION, AND THE REBORN CHILD

Seligman offers a simplified version of the story. He uses it as a rhetorical point to outline the three stages of human development: the camel, the lion, and the child. And we can also use this scheme for phases of personal development. Seligman has little to say about the camel, other than human history has for the greater part been in this stage: 'the camel just sits there and moans'. The second stage, the lion, is marked by political rebellion of almost 300 years of saying 'no' to the disabling condition of life such as poverty, racism, and disease. And commenting on the past 200 years of history, he argues, 'There is not only more wealth but also less racism, less pollution, more human rights, fewer battlefield deaths, more democracy, and on and on'. So, we all get to move on to the third stage, the child reborn. In this stage we say 'yes' to a more positive emotional life, yes to more engagement with others, yes to better relationships, yes to more meaning in life, and yes to more positive accomplishment, and we all say yes to human flourishing. It's a lovely thought, but devoid of reality.

By examining the story in greater detail it offers a more useful model for development.

A STORY OF THREE AWAKENINGS

From a more elaborate retelling, there are four characters and three transformations.[4] In this version, the actors are the spirit, the camel, the lion, and the child. And we can use this story for any aspect of our development, however small. Also, it is crucial to recognize that development is often not a linear or a serial process or even a holistic one. We might be at different stages for different aspects of our lives, and we might weave back and forth.

For any issue in life, you can ask 'Where am I?' in the arc of this story and decide what information, attitudes, and skills you need to move forward.

Preparations – a summary

The chapters of this book offer a set of resources to create the detail in each stage of your story. Here is a brief reminder of what we have covered:

- In the introduction, we set the parameters for the story using operational definitions – shared meaning.
- In 'Questions of trust' (Chapter 2), we considered a blueprint for critical thinking and to interrogate information for sources of error – obstacles to knowledge. We looked at the relationship between trust and truth, and between knowledge and empowerment. We also considered how knowledge and decision making are a balance of emotion and objectivity, and of intuition and experimentation.
- In 'Storytelling and sense-making' (Chapter 3), we looked at the stories we live by (narrative psychology) and how we structure our world using schemata. We developed our definition of the self by considering it as a bridge between the body and the social world. We addressed the question 'Who am I?' and how we related to wellbeing. Finally in this chapter we covered the issue of waking up to inequalities and their impact on health and wellbeing.
- In 'Stress and coping' (Chapter 4), we examined definitions of normality and looked at principles for positive mental health. We also explored stress from three angles (stimulus, response, and interaction) and how we might cope with it. The chapter introduced the idea of positive stress (eustress) to improve performance. It also offered ideas for getting support, and the uses and limits of mindfulness.
- In 'self-help and wellbeing' (Chapter 5), we explored the 'ifs, nots, myths, and knots' of the self-help movement. We looked at its origins and how the same themes repeat in the self-help genre. We also considered a strategy to choose and use a self-help book, in a way that puts you more in control.
- In 'Happiness, meaning, and the good life' (Chapter 6), we examined the contribution of positive psychology to our understanding of wellbeing. We looked at subjective wellbeing, flow, and models

of flourishing, criticisms of Positive psychology and pointers for ways forward.

The starting point – the spirit

The spirit (also called the sheep) stands for the stage in our development when we live passively, taking no risks, and look to avoid discomfort. We just get by.

And But there is still potential and to grow, the spirit needs to rise to new challenges with courage and power.

First transformation – from spirit to camel

The camel is a beast of burden, so has undertones of 'the dignity of labour' and the idea that hard work is all it takes. At this stage there's still an acceptance of the 'oughtness' and adjustment to the rules of the game. The camel has a sense of winning and 'staying in the game' with training and new learning.

To move to the next stage requires an awakening and questions that go beyond 'adjustment' (and conditioning), to questions of how things should and could be better.

Second transformation – from camel to lion

At this stage, the transformation can be the level of questioning and reassessing attitudes. At this stage there is a rejection of 'adjustment' to imposed limitations, obligations, stereotypes, and inequalities. But it requires more than a change of consciousness. Liberation needs action.

Third transformation – from lion to child

A child is constantly learning by spirit of experimentation, and in this sense the 'new normal' is forever renegotiated.

Sociologist Toffler in *Future Shock* talks about the need to learn, unlearn, and relearn.[5] And in Nietzsche's tale, transcendence follows. The idea of belonging to something greater than ourselves means we look beyond ourselves and to the impact we have on the wider world.

LITTLE BY LITTLE

To some, flourishing might seem a poetic and fanciful notion divorced from the sobering realities of everyday life. But we can achieve it by one act of resistance, one self-affirming goal, one small act of kindness and compassion, - one green shoot at a time. It is based on the traditional Tanzanian proverb I use with clients in coaching, 'Little by little, a little becomes a lot'.

So, finally . . .

Your wellbeing goals

Here's a brief exercise to set small, meaningful action steps in line with the concept of flow (Chapter 6). Use it in conjunction with above story. Pick a goal for any area of your life that might contribute to your wellbeing (or to make a contribution to others), and decide where are in the tale, and what you might need to edge you closer to the next stage.

- Rate your wellbeing on a scale from one to ten, with one being 'the lowest' and ten being 'the best it could be'.
- Why is it where it's at, and not lower? See this as an opportunity to take stock of what takes you up to this score, not to dwell on what's missing.
- What do you imagine doing at 0.5 along the scale? Write down as many small, meaningful, positive actions you can think of. Now do them. The review them. Then do some more.

P.S.

'I fully realize that I have not succeeded in answering all of your questions. . . . Indeed, I feel I have not answered any of them completely. The answers I have found only serve to raise a whole new set of questions, which only lead to more problems, some of which we weren't even aware were problems. To sum it all up. . . . In some ways I feel we are confused as ever, but I believe we are confused on a higher level, and about more important things'.[6]

FURTHER READING

BOOKS

Andreski, S. (1972). *Social Science as Sorcery*. London: Andre Deutsch.

Armstrong, K. (2010). *Twelve Steps to a Compassionate Life*. Maine: Thorndike Windsor Paragon.

Briers, S. (2012). *Psychobabble. Exploding the Myths of the self-Help Generation*. London: Pearson.

Csikszentmihalyi, M. (1997). *Finding Flow: The Psychology of Engagement with Everyday Life*. New York: Perseus Books.

Ehrenreich, B. (2009). *Smile or Die: How Positive Thinking Fooled America & the World*. London: Granta.

Grenville-Cleave, B. (2016). *Positive Psychology*. London: Icon Books.

Keyes, C.L.M. & Haidt, J. (2002). *Flourishing: Positive Psychology and the Life Well-Lived*. Washington: American Psychological Association.

Lilienfeld, S.O., Lynn, S.J., Ruscio, J. & Beyerstein, B.L. (2010). *50 Great Myths of Popular Psychology. Shattering Widespread Misconceptions about Human Behaviour*. Chichester: Wiley-Blackwell.

Lindner, R. (1971). *The Revolutionist's Handbook*. New York: Grove Press.

Rotenberg, K.J. (2018). *The Psychology of Trust*. London & New York: Routledge.

Salerno, S. (2005). *SHAM. How the Gurus of the Self-Help Movement Make Us Helpless*. London & Boston: Nicholas Brealey.

Seligman, M. (2011). *Flourish: A New Understanding of Happiness and Wellbeing: The Practical Guide to Using Positive Psychology to Make You Happier and Healthier*. London: Nicholas Brealey.

Watzlawick, P. (1993). *The Situation Is Hopeless, but Not Serious: The Pursuit of Unhappiness*. London: W.W. Norton & Company.

Wilkinson, R. & Pickett, K. (2009). *The Spirit Level: Why More Equal Societies Almost Always Do Better*. London: Allen Lane.

Wood, G.W. (2013). *Unlock Your Confidence*. London: Watkins Books.

Wood, G.W, (2018). The *Psychology of Gender*. London & New York: Routledge.

Wood, G.W. (2019). *Letters to a New Student. Tips to Study Smarter from a Psychologist*. London & New York: Routledge.

NOVELS

Inspirational

Illusions: The Adventures of a Reluctant Messiah by Richard Bach. Arrow Books, 2001.
Jonathan Livingston Seagull: A Story by Richard Bach. Harper Collins, 1994.
The Little Prince by Antoine de Saint-Exupéry (Kathryn Woods translation). Picador, 1982.

Dystopian

Nineteen Eighty-Four (1984) by George Orwell/ Penguin Modern Classics, 2004 (originally 1949).

Fahrenheit 451 by Ray Bradbury. Flamingo Modern Classics, 1999 (originally 1953).

Swastika Night by Katharine Burdekin. The Feminist Press, 1985 (Originally 1937).

FILMS

Big Fish (2003, directed by Tim Burton).
Life Is Beautiful (1999, directed by Roberto Benigni).
Pleasantville (1998, directed by Gary Ross).

WEBSITES

For a range of copyright free psychometric measures on subjective wellbeing visit: https://eddiener.com/scales

To discover your values and character strengths visit: www.viacharacter.org/

Read, affirm and share the 'Charter for Compassion': https://charterforcompassion.org/charter/affirm

To get in touch with the author to discuss coaching and research email: info@drgarywood.co.uk. Or visit: www.drgarywood.co.uk

NOTES

PREFACE

1 Simon, W. (1996). *Postmodern Sexualities*. London: Routledge, p.1.

2 Or, in response to a journalist about tips for wellbeing, I replied 'Don't write a book about it'.

3 Probably, the worse episode, ever.

4 Yes, call me 'lucky Gary'. The lump turned out to be a mild infection, which I cleared up by a few hot compresses – before I got to see a doctor.

5 I had to reflect on this question after reading Parker, I. (2020). *Psychology through Critical Auto-Ethnography*. London & New York: Routledge.

6 Who wrote "A writer only begins a book. A reader finishes it."? Skeptics. https://skeptics.stackexchange.com/questions/44068/who-wrote-a-writer-only-begins-a-book-a-reader-finishes-it/ Accessed 3/3/2020.

7 I recall a guest lecture, while a student, by a psychiatrist Sashi Sashidharan. He opened with the line that he had now read 75% of the material he regularly cites. At that moment we all felt busted.

8 When new coaching clients swear for the first time in a session, they at once apologize. I usually tell them, it's important for them to be authentic, and I add that 'swearing is my hobby'. That usually lightens the mood.

9 Known by the mononym 'Brown' – his surname.

10 Wood, G. (2008). *Don't Wait for Your Ship to Come In . . . Swim Out to Meet It!* Chichester: Capstone.

11 As defined by the psychometric test The Political Compass, see: https://

www.politicalcompass.org/. It's a way of saying 'democratic socialist' without people losing their shit.

12 Crossed-out (sous rature = under erasure) – after philosopher Martin Heidegger (1889–1976) – to signify that this categorization is inadequate but necessary. See: Taylor, V.E. & Winquist, C.E. (2001). *Encyclopaedia of Postmodernism*. London: Taylor & Francis, p. 113. Also used by philosopher Jacques Derrida (1930–2004).

13 Although, I do not dispute that some aspects of the genetic lottery have conferred advantages.

14 See: Bornstein, K. (1998). *My Gender Workbook*. New York & London: Routledge. As for pronouns, I use 'he/him' in writing, but psychologically I'm more they/them, but have no objection to she/her. I now joke that my personal pronoun is 'it' – with a silent Q. Again. I view pronouns as 'inadequate but necessary'. See note 12.

15 A reference to the song 'Sport (The Odd Boy)' written by Vivian Stanshall. From the 1969 album Keynsham by performed by The Bonzo Dog (Doo Dah) Band.

16 Three years earlier, my list was much the same list, just in a different order. If you'd like to take the test for yourself, visit: https://www.viacharacter.org/

17 He goes on to say, 'and can hardly fail to be dubbed as an obnoxious heretic or a dangerous subversive', See: Andreski, S. (1972). *Social Sciences as Sorcery*. London: Andre Deutsch, p.104. I should be so lucky!

18 I don't remember who said it to me, but it looks like a paraphrase of a quotation by poet and philosopher Paul Valéry (1871–1945): 'A poem is never finished, only abandoned.' See: https://www.goodreads.com/author/quotes/141425.Paul_Val_ry. Accessed 7/3/2020.

CHAPTER 1

1 The Vulcan greeting and salute, 'Live long and prosper', created by actor Leonard Nimoy in *StarTrek*. See: https://archive.li/3bK5. Accessed 3/8/2019 (using the D/M/Y convention).

2 Yes, I have opted for the closed version, as it has become standard in the UK. Also, I was surprised to find several references to 'wellbeing' in online bookshops. For a discussion of different spellings see: https://grammarist.com/spelling/well-being-wellbeing/. Accessed 3/8/2019.

3 See: https://globalwellnessinstitute.org/press-room/press-releases/wellness-now-a-4-2-trillion-global-industry/. Accessed 14/7/2019.

4   Morin, A. (2019). How to Improve Your Psychological Well-Being. *VeryWell Mind*. www.verywellmind.com/improve-psychological-well-being-4177330. Accessed 19/1/2020.

5   Deacon, M. (2016). Michael Gove's Guide to Britain's Greatest Enemy . . . the Experts. *The Telegraph*. www.telegraph.co.uk/news/2016/06/10/michael-goves-guide-to-britains-greatest-enemy-the-experts/. Accessed 13/6/2019. See also: Deb, S. (2016). Trump: 'The Experts Are Terrible'. *CBS News*. www.cbsnews.com/news/trump-the-experts-are-terrible/. Accessed 13/6/2019.

6   Referring to the Karen 'memes' on Facebook. For gender balance you might add 'Kevin' on Twitter.

7   'They say' is often used to preface arguments.

8   Short for popular psychology.

9   Like 'giving a fish' versus 'teaching fishing', as the well-worn proverb goes.

10 Known as 'operational definitions'.

11 When learning, we work from the familiar towards the unfamiliar and from the concrete to the abstract. That's why the book the starts with your own experience: Wood, G.W. (2019). *Letters to a New Student. Tips to Study Smarter from a Psychologist*. London & New York: Routledge.

12 Rest assured: this is not an inspirational self-help book. I won't ask you to howl at the moon, at midnight, dancing naked, on top of a hill, offering up a pink balloon to the universe. Unless that's your thing.

13 Many hilarious, Basil-Fawlty-like exchanges followed during our stay. My favourite line of the holiday was 'I won't make you an omelette and my estranged wife won't make you one either!'

14 Polonius in Shakespeare's *Hamlet* (Act 1, Scene III) says, 'This above all: to thine own self be true'. In the play it's about 'looking after number one' rather than today's call to individuality. Other examples include the famous maxim 'Know yourself' (or 'Be yourself') inscribed at the Temple of Apollo at Delphi and Madonna's call to 'Express Yourself'.

15 Bee (1992) cited in McLeod, S. (2008). Self-Concept. *Simply Psychology* see: www.simplypsychology.org/self-concept.html. Accessed 4/11/2019.

16 McLeod (2008).

17 Dennett, D.C. (1992). The self as a Center of Narrative Gravity. In: F. Kessel, P. Cole & D. Johnson (eds.) *Self and Consciousness: Multiple Perspectives*. Hillsdale, NJ: Erlbaum. See: http://cogprints.org/266/1/selfctr.htm. Accessed 5/7/2019.

18 See: Sedikides, C. & Spencer, S.J. (Eds.) (2007). *The self*. New York: Psychology Press.

19 Dodge, R., Daly, A., Huyton, J. & Sanders, L. (2012). The Challenge of Defining Wellbeing. *International Journal of Wellbeing*, 2 (3), 222–235. -0.5502/ijw. v2i3.4. Accessed 5/1/2020.

20 Davis, T. (2019). What Is Well-Being? Definition, Types, and Well-Being Skills. *Psychology Today*. See: www.psychologytoday.com/us/blog/click-here-happiness/201901/what-is-well-being-definition-types-and-well-being-skills. Accessed 8/1/2020.

21 Dodge et al. (2012). This is my paraphrase, not a direct quotation.

22 See: the British Psychological Society (BPS): www.bps.org.uk. See also: the American Psychological Association (APA): www.apa.org/ Accessed 28/6/2019.

23 Using more than one way to look at things from different angles is known as triangulation.

24 From his most famous play *The Importance of Being Earnest*, in 1895.

25 I expect you're annoyed now at jumping to this endnote only to find it is useless. Damn you experts!

26 Although all we manage to achieve is 'bounded subjectivity'. See: Wood, G.W. (2000). *Intolerance of Ambiguity, Gender Stereotypes, and Attitudes to Sexuality*. Unpublished PhD Thesis. Birmingham: Aston University.

27 Reynold, D.K. (1982). *The Quiet Therapies. Japanese Pathways to Personal Growth*. Honolulu: University of Hawaii Press.

28 The Psychology of Everything series aims to bridge the gap between academic and pop psychology, written more in the active voice and in first person but with an evidence-based approach.

29 The statement 'if I have seen further, it is by standing on the shoulders of giants' is by Isaac Newton (1642–1727), mathematician, physicist, astronomer, theologian, and author. See: https://discover.hsp.org/Record/dc-9792/Description#tabnav. Accessed 28/6/2019.

30 See: Rosnow, R.L. (1997). *People Studying People. Artifacts and Ethics in Behavioral Research*. New York: W.H. Freeman & Company.

31 Hamby, S. (2018). Know Thyself: How to Write a Reflexivity Statement. *Psychology Today*. See: www.psychologytoday.com/us/blog/the-web-violence/201805/know-thyself-how-write-reflexivity-statement. Accessed 17/1/2020.

32 Wood (2019).

CHAPTER 2

1 Ries & Trout (1981) cited in Pratkanis, A. & Aronson, E. (2001). *Age of Propaganda. The Everyday Use and Abuse of Persuasion* (Rev. ed.). New York: Owl Books.

2 Fredrickson, B.L. (2004). The Broaden-and-build Theory of Positive Emotions. *Philosophical Transactions of the Royal Society of London*, 359 (1449), pp. 1367–1378. See: www.ncbi.nlm.nih.gov/pmc/articles/PMC1693418/pdf/15347528.pdf. Accessed 19/3/2020.

3 Wolf, M. (2018). Skim Reading Is the New Normal. The Effect on Society Is Profound. *The Guardian*. See: www.theguardian.com/commentisfree/2018/aug/25/skim-reading-new-normal-maryanne-wolf. Accessed 9/3/2020.

4 Braynov, S. & Sandholm, T. (2002). Incentive Compatible Mechanism for Trust Revelation. AAMAS'02. See: www.csee.umbc.edu/~msmith27/read ings/protected/braynov-2002a.pdf. Accessed 8/3/2020. Also: Rotenberg, K.J. (2018). *The Psychology of Trust*. London & New York: Routledge, p. 1.

5 Edelman (2020). *Trust Barometer*, See: www.edelman.com/trustbarometer. Accessed 9/3/2020.

6 Humanists UK (no date). Religion and Belief: Some Surveys and Statistics. https://humanism.org.uk/campaigns/religion-and-belief-some-surveys-and-statistics/. Accessed 27/3/2020.

7 Gaiman, N. (2001). *American Gods*. London: Headline.

8 Pluckrose, H. (2017). The Problem with Truth and Reason in a Post-Truth Society. *Areo Magazine*. See: https://areomagazine.com/2017/12/08/the-prob lem-with-truth-and-reason-in-a-post-truth-society/. Accessed 9/3/2020. Wedge, M. (2017). The Historical Origin of 'Alternative Facts'. *Psychology Today*. www.psychologytoday.com/us/blog/suffer-the-children/201701/the-his torical-origin-alternative-facts. Accessed 5/4/2020.

9 The Spectator (2017). *Keeping Faith*. See: www.spectator.co.uk/article/keep ing-faith-7-september-2017. Accessed 9/3/2020.

10 Edelman (2020).

11 Edelman (2015) cited in Rotenberg (2018), p. 1.

12 Clench, S. (2020). Coronavirus: Donald Trump Changes Attitude After Down-playing the Virus for Months. *News.com.au*. See: www.news.com.au/finance/economy/world-economy/donald-trump-announces-massive-coronavi rus-package/news-story/6c7a5e33fb842d9c05d1601e6427a564. Accessed 20/3/2020. Abraham, T. (2020). China's Response to the Coronavi rus Shows What It Learned from the Sars Cover-up. *The Guardian*. www.theguard ian.com/global/commentisfree/2020/jan/23/china-coronavirus-sars-cov er-up-beijing-disease-dissent. Accessed 20/3/2020. 'Big Ben Bongs' Refers to Great Bell in the Elisabeth Bell Tower at the Palace of Westminster in Lon-don. See: Wharton, J. (2020). Cash Raised for Big Ben Brexit Bong Can't Be Spent on Ringing Bell. *The Metro*. https://metro.co.uk/2020/01/17/cash-raised-big-ben-brexit-bong-cant-spent-ringing-bell-12073465/. Accessed 20/3/2020.

13 Graham-Harrison, E. (2020). Coronavirus: How Asian Countries Acted While the West Dithered. *The Guardian*. www.theguardian.com/world/2020/mar/21/coronavirus-asia-acted-west-dithered-hong-kong-taiwan-europe.

Accessed 10/5/2020. Bicker, L. (2020). Coronavirus in South Korea: How 'Trace, Test and Treat' May Be Saving Lives. *BBC News*. www.bbc.co.uk/news/world-asia-51836898. Accessed 30/3/2020.

14 Duffy, N. (2020). Coronavirus in the UK: Public Health Experts and Political Opponents Call on Government to Share Modelling. *i News*. See: https://inews.co.uk/news/health/coronavirus-covid-19-uk-public-health-data-models-government-jeremy-corbyn-2450646. Accessed 28/3/2020.

15 Huang, Y. (2020). U.S.-Chinese Distrust Is Inviting Dangerous Coronavirus Conspiracy Theories. *Foreign Affairs*. See: www.foreignaffairs.com/articles/united-states/2020-03-05/us-chinese-distrust-inviting-dangerous-coronavirus-conspiracy. Accessed 29/3/2020. Also: Feuer, W. (2020). 'Confusion Breeds Distrust': China Keeps Changing How It Counts Coronavirus Cases. *CNBC*. See: www.cnbc.com/2020/02/26/confusion-breeds-distrust-china-keeps-changing-how-it-counts-coronavirus-cases.html. Accessed 29/3/2020.

16 Wood, G.W. (2018). *The Psychology of Gender*. London & New York: Routledge.

17 Connell, R. & Pearse, R. (2014). *Gender: In World Perspective*. Cambridge: Polity Press.

18 Taub, A. (2020). Why Are Women-Led Nations Doing Better With Covid-19? New York Times. See: https://www.nytimes.com/2020/05/15/world/coronavirus-women-leaders.html. Accessed 10/7/2020. Brannon, R. (1976). The Male Sex Role: Our Culture's Blueprint of Manhood, and What It's Done for Us Lately. In: Deborah S. David & Robert Brannon (eds.) *The Forty-Nine Percent Majority: The Male Sex Role*. Reading, MA: Addison-Wesley, pp. 14–15, 30–32. And for an analysis of military masculinity see: http://digitalhumanities.unl.edu/resources/students/blocke/militarymasculinitycomplex/intro.html. Accessed 29/3/2020.

19 Taber, J.M., Leyva, B. & Persoskie, A. (2014). Why Do People Avoid Medical Care? A Qualitative Study Using National Data. *Journal of Internal Medicine*, 30 (3), pp. 290–297. See: www.ncbi.nlm.nih.gov/pmc/articles/PMC4351276/.

20 Lickerman, A. (2013). When Patients Refuse Their Doctors' Advice. *Psychology Today*. www.psychologytoday.com/us/blog/happiness-in-world/201311/when-patients-refuse-their-doctors-advice. Accessed 28/3/2020.

21 Luciani, J. (2012). 6 Reasons We Ignore the Doctor's Advice (And Why We Shouldn't). *HuffPost*. See: www.huffpost.com/entry/ignore-doctor-advice_n_1262643. Accessed 28/3/2020.

22 See also: Tasler, N. (2013). Why We Ignore Good Advice. *Psychology Today*. See: www.psychologytoday.com/us/blog/strategic-thinking/201303/why-we-ignore-good-advice. Accessed 28/3/2020. Vlassoff, C. (2007). Gender Differences

in Determinants and Consequences of Health and Illness. *Journal of Health, Population, and Nutrition*, 25 (1), pp. 47–61. Koven, S. (2013). Why Patients Don't Always Follow Doctor's Orders. *Boston Globe*. See: www.bostonglobe.com/life style/health-wellness/2013/04/21/practice-why-patients-don-always-fol low-orders/6HRxBeEuLf7jCk2pu7iIKP/story.html. Accessed 28/3/2020.

23 Erikson (1963) cited in Wrightsman, L.S. (1992). *Assumptions About Human Nature. Implications for Researchers and Practitioners* (2nd ed.). London: Sage, p. 202.

24 Dodge et al. (2012). This is my paraphrase, not a direct quotation.

25 Carrington, D. (2018). BBC Admits 'We Get Climate Change Coverage Wrong Too Often'. *The Guardian*. See: www.theguardian.com/environment/2018/sep/07/bbc-we-get-climate-change-coverage-wrong-too-often. Accessed 4/4/2020.

26 Proctor, K. (2020).UK Anti-Fake News Unit Dealing With Up to 10 False Coronavirus Articles a Day. *The Guardian*. www.theguardian.com/world/2020/mar/30/uk-anti-fake-news-unit-coronavirus. Accessed 5/4/2020.

27 Proctor (2020). The website was WND.com, rated far right and mixed factual reporting. See: https://mediabiasfactcheck.com/world-net-daily-wnd/. Accessed 5/4/2020.

28 Waterson, J. (2020).UK Media Outlets Told Not to Promote Baseless 5G Coronavirus Theories. *The Guardian*. See: www.theguardian.com/media/2020/apr/02/uk-media-outlets-told-not-to-promote-baseless-5g-coronavirus-theories. Accessed 4/4/2020.

29 Van Prooijen, J-W. (2018). *The Psychology of Conspiracy Theories*. London & New York: Routledge.

30 Beckett, C. (2015). How Journalism Is Turning Emotional and What That Might Mean for News. *LSE Blog*. https://blogs.lse.ac.uk/polis/2015/09/10/how-journalism-is-turning-emotional-and-what-that-might-mean-for-news/. Accessed 4/4/2020.

31 Beckett (2015). n.p. (it refers to a Internet article so there's no page number).

32 See: The Assassin's Creed Wiki | Fandom: https://assassinscreed.fandom.com/wiki/The_Creed. Accessed 6/4/2020. For the origins of the maxim, see: Art and Popular Culture Encyclopaedia: www.artandpopularculture.com/Nothing_is_true%2C_everything_is_permitted. Accessed 6/4/2020.

33 Waterson (2020).

34 Binns, A. (2017). Online Trolls Mustn't Be Allowed To Intimidate Journalists. *The Conversation*. See: https://theconversation.com/online-trolls-mustnt-be-allowed-to-intimidate-journalists-80531. Accessed 5/4/2020. And: Delgado, K. (2015). Why Is Robert Peston's Hair More Important Than It

Sounds? *Radio Times*. See: www.radiotimes.com/news/2015-02-11/why-is-robert-pestons-hair-more-important-than-it-sounds/. Accessed 6/4/2020.

35 Bunz, M. (2010). Most Journalists Use Social Media Such as Twitter and Facebook as a Source. *The Guardian*. See: www.theguardian.com/media/pda/2010/feb/15/journalists-social-music-twitter-facebook. Accessed 6/4/2020.

36 *The Week* (2019). Is the UK media's Election Coverage Fair? www.theweek.co.uk/104428/is-the-uk-media-s-election-coverage-fair. Accessed 31/3/2020.

37 Tweet by Michael Rosen on 7/11/2019: https://twitter.com/MichaelRosenYes/status/1192559543068307468. Accessed 23/1/2020. The tweet was in the context of negative coverage of the Labour leader Jeremy Corbyn.

38 Pinborough, S. (2017). Top 10 Unreliable Narrators. *The Guardian*. See: www.theguardian.com/books/2017/jan/04/top-10-unreliable-narrators-edgar-allan-poe-gillian-flynn. Accessed 4/4/2020.

39 Video: Peter Oborne names and shames BBC and ITV journalists spreading fake news. See: https://youtu.be/yX_wug7B7AM. Accessed 4/4/2020. See also: Oborne, P. (2019). British Journalists Have Become Part of Johnson's Fake News Machine. *Open Democracy*. See: www.opendemocracy.net/en/opendemocracyuk/british-journalists-have-become-part-of-johnsons-fake-news-machine/. Accessed 4/4/2020.

40 *The Daily Mail* is rated right-wing with low factual reporting and considered untrustworthy. See: https://mediabiasfactcheck.com/daily-mail/. Accessed 4/4/2020. *The Daily Telegraph* is rated right-wing and 'mixed' for factual reporting. See: https://mediabiasfactcheck.com/daily-telegraph/. Accessed 4/4/2020.

41 Oborne, P. (2019).

42 Jonathan Foster, personal communication, 28/3/2020. In my email, I did replace the expletive with '*******'. His reply: 'It's inaccurate. Its source, however, is the third-year journalism skills module at the University of Sheffield. What you cite is a composite of axioms – some mine (I was the tutor in charge of the course) and one from my former 'Observer' colleague, Nick Davies, who was a guest lecturer. Neither of us would have said 'your job is to look out the window'.

43 Oscar Wilde (1854–1900), poet, playwright, and author.

44 Tornoe, R. (2018). Trump to Veterans: Don't Believe What You're Reading or Seeing. *The Philadelphia Inquirer*. See: www.inquirer.com/philly/news/politics/presidential/donald-trump-vfw-speech-kansas-city-what-youre-seeing-reading-not-whats-happening-20180724.html. Accessed 1/4/2020. George Orwell's 1984 has the line, 'The Party told you to reject the evidence of your eyes and ears. It was their final, most essential command'. See: https://genius.com/George-orwell-nineteen-eighty-four-book-1-chapter-7-annotated. Accessed 4/4/2020.

45 Friedman, U. (2017). Why Trump Is Thriving in an Age of Distrust. *The Atlantic*. See: www.theatlantic.com/international/archive/2017/01/trumpedel man-trust-crisis/513350/. Accessed 11/4/2020.

46 Vosoughi, S., Roy, D. & Aral, S. (2018). The Spread of True and False News Online. *Science*, 359, 6380, pp. 1146–1151. https://science.sciencemag.org/content/359/6380/1146. Accessed 6/4/2020.

47 The Real Story of 'Fake News'. Merriam-Webster Dictionary. See: www.merriam-webster.com/words-at-play/the-real-story-of-fake-news. Accessed 6/4/2020.

48 Murphy, M. (2018). Government Bans Phrase 'Fake News'. *The Telegraph*. www.telegraph.co.uk/technology/2018/10/22/government-bans-phrase-fake-news/. Accessed 6/4/2020.

49 Wardle, C. (2017). Fake News. It's Complicated. *First Draft*. See: https://first draftnews.org/latest/fake-news-complicated/. Accessed 4/4/2020.

50 Lind, D. (2018). President Donald Trump Finally Admits That 'Fake News' Just Means News He Doesn't Like. *Vox*. www.vox.com/policy-and-politics/2018/5/9/17335306/trump-tweet-twitter-latest-fake-news-credentials. Accessed 6/4/2020.

51 Griffin, A. (2019). General Election: Almost Every Tory Ad Dishonest, Compared with None of Labour's, Research Finds. *The Independent*. www.independent.co.uk/life-style/gadgets-and-tech/news/general-election-bo ris-johnson-conservatives-labour-corbyn-facebook-ads-a9241781.html. Accessed 6/4/2020.

52 Forster, K. (2017). Revealed: How Dangerous Fake Health News Conquered Facebook. *The Independent*. See: www.independent.co.uk/life-style/health-and-families/health-news/fake-news-health-facebook-cruel-damag ing-social-media-mike-adams-natural-health-ranger-conspiracy-a7498201.html. Accessed 6/4/2020.

53 Naughton, J. (2020). Fake News About Covid-19 Can Be as Dangerous as the Virus. *The Guardian*. www.theguardian.com/commentisfree/2020/mar/14/fake-news-about-covid-19-can-be-as-dangerous-as-the-virus. Accessed 7/4/2020.

54 Vosoughi et al (2018).

55 Chadwick, P. (2020). Why Fake News on Social Media Travels Faster Than the Truth. *The Guardian*. See: www.theguardian.com/commentisfree/2018/mar/19/fake-news-social-media-twitter-mit-journalism. Accessed 6/4/2020.

56 Video: Noam Chomsky 2017 | Talks at Google see: www.youtube.com/watch?v=2C-zWrhFqpM. Accessed 7/4/2020. View from 53:00.

57 Naughton (2020).

58 'Same Time Tomorrow' by Laurie Anderson from her 1994 album *Bright Red* on Warner Brothers.

59 Fyodor Mikhailovich Dostoevsky (1821–1881). See: Encyclopaedia Britannica. www.britannica.com/biography/Fyodor-Dostoyevsky. Accessed 1/4/2020.

60 See: www.eonline.com/shows/botched. Accessed 3/4/2020.

61 There's also an element of beating the system.

62 www.realself.com/article/common-mistakes-choosing-plastic-surgeon.

63 Furnham, A. & Levitas, J. (2012). Factors That Motivate People to Undergo Cosmetic Surgery. *The Canadian Journal of Plastic Surgery*, 20 (4), pp. e47–e50. See: www.ncbi.nlm.nih.gov/pmc/articles/PMC3513261/. Accessed 3/4/2020. And: Abbas, O.L. & Karadavut, U. (2017). Analysis of the Factors Affecting Men's Attitudes Toward Cosmetic Surgery: Body Image, Media Exposure, Social Network Use, Masculine Gender Role Stress and Religious Attitudes. *Aesthetic Plastic Surgery*, 41 (6), pp. 1454–1462. See: www.ncbi.nlm.nih.gov/pubmed/28451800. Accessed 3/4/2020.

64 Abraham, A. & Zuckerman, D. (2011). Adolescents, Celebrity Worship, and Cosmetic Surgery. *Journal of Adolescent Health*, 49 (5), pp. 453–454. See: www.jahonline.org/article/S1054-139X(11)00302-8/fulltext. Accessed 3/4/2020.

65 BAAPS Consumer Safety Guidelines. British Association of Aesthetic Plastic Surgeons See: https://baaps.org.uk/patients/safety_in_surgery/consumer_safety_guidelines.aspx. Accessed 3/4/2020.

66 Hackett, J. (2015). Roger Bacon. In Edward N. Zalta (ed.) *The Stanford Encyclopedia of Philosophy* (Spring 2015 ed.). See: https://plato.stanford.edu/archives/spr2015/entries/roger-bacon. Accessed 8/4/2020.

67 Hackett (2015).

68 Shermer (2011) cited in Van Prooijen (2018).

69 Van Prooijen (2018).

70 Martel et al. (2019), and Bago et al. (2019) cited in: Pennycook, G., McPhetres, J., Zhang, Y. & Rand, D. (2020). Fighting COVID-19 Misinformation on Social Media: Experimental Evidence for a Scalable Accuracy Nudge Intervention. See: https://psyarxiv.com/uhbk9/. Accessed 13/4/2020.

71 Beckett (2015) and Heshmat, S. (2015). What Is Confirmation Bias? *Psychology Today*. See: www.psychologytoday.com/us/blog/science-choice/201504/what-is-confirmation-bias. Accessed 10/4/2020.

72 See: Cambridge definition of experiment: https://dictionary.cambridge.org/dictionary/english/experiment. Accessed 13/4/2020.

73 Friedrich Nietzsche from The Joyful Wisdom, p. 78. See: https://archive.org/details/completenietasch10nietuoft/page/78/mode/2up. Accessed 13/4/2020.

74 Edelman (2020).

75 King, B.S. (2017). The Real Dunning-Kruger Graph. *Graph Paper Diaries*. See: https://graphpaperdiaries.com/2017/08/20/the-real-dunning-kruger-graph/. Accessed 10/4/2020.

76 Roger Bacon (c.1219/20–c.1292) cited in Andreski (1972), p. 8. See also: Smith, R. (2017). Richard Smith: Roger Bacon on Ignorance and Peer Review. *The BMJ Opinion*. https://blogs.bmj.com/bmj/2017/05/04/richard-smith-roger-bacon-on-ignorance-and-peer-review/. Accessed 9/9/2019. For the various translations check out http://www2.hawaii.edu/~daniel/bacon.html. Accessed 20/9/2019.

77 See: http://www2.hawaii.edu/~daniel/bacon.html. Accessed 8/4/2020.

78 CPS (2019). CPS Guidance for Experts on Disclosure, Unused Material and Case Management. See: www.cps.gov.uk/legal-guidance/cps-guidance-experts-disclosure-unused-material-and-case-management. Accessed 14/4/2020.

79 Wood (2018).

80 Definition from Merriam-Webster. See: www.merriam-webster.com/dictionary/custom. Accessed 16/4/2020.

81 Prager is quoted in Lilienfeld, S.O., Lynn, S.J., Ruscio, J. & Beyerstein, B.L. (2010). *50 Great Myths of Popular Psychology*. Chichester: Wiley-Blackwell, p. 5.

82 Gardner, E. (2018). Conservative Video Producer Suing Google Over 'Censorship' Pushes for Injunction. *The Hollywood Reporter*. See: www.hollywoodreporter.com/thr-esq/conservative-video-producer-suing-google-censorship-pushes-injunction-1070959. Accessed 2/4/2020.

83 Prager (2002) cited in Lilienfeld et al. (2010), p. 5.

84 Asimov, I. (1980). A Cult of Ignorance. *Newsweek*, 21 January, p. 19.

85 Goldberg, S. (2019). On Being Entitled to One's Opinion. Cardiff University. *Blogs for Open Debate*. See: https://blogs.cardiff.ac.uk/openfordebate/2019/02/11/on-being-entitled-to-ones-opinion/. Accessed 12/4/2020.

86 Allem, J-P. (2010). Social Media Fuels Wave of Coronavirus Misinformation as Users Focus on Popularity, Not Accuracy. *The Conversation*. See: https://theconversation.com/social-media-fuels-wave-of-coronavirus-misinformation-as-users-focus-on-popularity-not-accuracy-135179. Accessed 13/4/2020. And: Pennycook et al. (2020).

87 Such as Snopes.com, Fullfact.org, and Mediabiasfactcheck.com.

88 Majmundar, A., Allem, J-P., Cruz, T.B. & Unger, J.B. (2018).The Why We Retweet Scale. *PLOS One*. See: https://journals.plos.org/plosone/article?id=10.1371/journal.pone.0206076. Accessed 13/4/2020.

89 Boynton, P.N., Wood, G.W. & Greenhalgh, T. (2004). Hands-on Guide to Questionnaire Research. Reaching Beyond the White Middle Classes. *BMJ,*

328 (7453), pp. 1433–1436. See: www.ncbi.nlm.nih.gov/pmc/articles/PMC421793/. Accessed 14/4/2020.

90 Shouhayib, J. (2015). What Can Psychology Tell Us About Racism? *American Psychological Association*. See: www.apa.org/pi/about/newsletter/2015/12/racism-psychology. Accessed 15/4/2020. And: Supple, S. (2005). Disability – Special Issue. *The Psychologist*. See: https://thepsychologist.bps.org.uk/volume-18/edition-7/disability-special-issue. Accessed 16/4/2020.

91 Wood, G.W. (2019). *Letters to a New Student. Tips to Study Smarter from Psychologist*. London & New York: Routledge, p. 85.

92 Andreski, S. (1972). *Social Science a Sorcery*. London: Andre Deutsch. p.32, p.59.

93 Video: Boris Johnson explains how to speak like Winston Churchill. www.youtube.com/watch?v=FLak2IzIv7U&t=106s. Accessed 1/4/2020. Video: Boris Johnson tests Evan Davis's Latin – BBC Newsnight. See: www.youtube.com/watch?v=oJXyI-gwBNU. Accessed 1/4/2020. Johnson, B. (2015). *The Churchill Factor: How One Man Made History*. London: Hodder.

94 McKay, B. & McKay, K. (2015, 2018). The Winston Churchill Guide to Public Speaking. *Art of Manliness*. See: www.artofmanliness.com/articles/guide-to-public-speaking/. Accessed 7/4/2020.

95 Quoted in: Quoted in: Clayton, V. (2015). The Needless Complexity of Academic Writing. *The Atlantic*. See: www.theatlantic.com/education/archive/2015/10/complex-academic-writing/412255/. Accessed 2/4/2020.

96 Wood (2019).

97 James, M. (2014–2020). Evaluation of Sources. *History Skills*. See: www.historyskills.com/source-criticism/evaluation/. Accessed 16/4/2020. And Stainton-Rogers & Stainton-Rogers (2001).

98 Stainton-Rogers & Stainton-Rogers (2001). Tony Benn (1925–2014) was a British politician and diarist. See: Nichols, J. (2014). Tony Benn and the Five Essential Questions of Democracy. *The Nation*. See: www.thenation.com/article/tony-benn-and-five-essential-questions-democracy/ Accessed 13/6/2019.

99 Rotenberg (2018); Barefoot et al. (1998) cited in Rotenberg (2018); Fuertes et al. (2007) cited in Rotenberg (2018).

CHAPTER 3

1 Sarbin, Theodore R. (1986). *Narrative Psychology: The Storied Nature of Human Conduct*. Santa Barbara, CA: Praeger.

2 Cron, L. (2012). *Wired for Story: The Writer's Guide to Using Brain Science to Hook Readers from the Very First Sentence*. CA: Ten Speed Press, p. 1.

3 Hoffman, R.J. (1984). Vices, Gods and Virtues: Cosmology as a Mediating Force in Attitudes to Homosexuality. *Journal of Homosexuality*, 9, pp. 27–44.

4 Grayling, A.C. (2002). Scientist or Storyteller? *The Guardian*. See: www.theguard ian.com/books/2002/jun/22/socialsciences.gender. Accessed 20/2/2020.

5 Scarry, E. (1985). *The Body in Pain. The Making and Unmaking of the World*. Oxford: Oxford University Press. And: Wood, G.W. (2018). *The Psychology of Gender*. Oxford: Routledge, p.81.

6 Hardy, B. (2013). *Tellers and Listeners: The Narrative Imagination*. London: Blooms-bury Academic. And: Hardy (1977) cited in Snyder, I. (2006). New Media and Cultural Form: Narrative Versus Database. See: www.craigbellamy. net/2006/10/26/new-media-and-cultural-form-narrative-versus-data base/. Accessed 18/2/2020.

7 Rosen, M. (2016). Michael Rosen on the Power of Storytelling. *Country Living*. www.countryliving.com/uk/wellbeing/a1202/michael-rosen-power-of-storytelling/ Accessed 28/1/2020.

8 Parker, I. (1994). Preface. In: P. Bannister, E. Burman, I. Parker, M. Taylor & C. Tindall (1994). *Qualitative Methods in Psychology. A Research Guide*. Buckingham: Open University Press, pp. 2–3.

9 The version I saw had no author details.

10 Beck, J. (2015). Life's Stories. How You Arrange the Plot Points of Your Life into a Narrative Can Shape Who You Are – and Is a Fundamental. *The Atlantic*. www. theatlantic.com/health/archive/2015/08/life-stories-narrative-psychology-redemption-mental-health/400796/ Accessed 23/1/2020. Greenhalgh, T. & Hurwitz, B. (1998). Why Study Narrative? In: T. Greenhalgh & B. Hurwitz (eds.) *Narrative Based Medicine*. London: BMJ Books. Reynolds, R. (1984). *Playing Ball on Running Water. A Unique Japanese Guide to Getting More Out of Life*. London: Sheldon Press.

11 Beck (2015). Aaker & Aaker (2016) cited in Fielder, P. (2018). Why Your Brand Needs a Signature Story and How to Tell It. *Medium*. See: https://medium. com/better-marketing/signaturestory-7bcec7faaedb. Accessed 05/2/2020. Also: Briers, S. (2012). *Psychobabble. Exploding the Myths of the self-Help Generation*. Harlow: Pearson Education, p. 73.

12 Quoted in Beck (2015).

13 Mulkay (1985) cited in Stainton-Rogers, W. & Stainton-Rogers, R. (2001). *The Psychology of Gender and Sexuality*. Buckingham: Open University Press, p. 197.

14 Bort, R. (2019). Obama Calls Out Online Call-Out Culture: 'That's Not Activism'. *Rolling Stone*. www.rollingstone.com/politics/politics-news/obama-calls-out-call-out-culture-not-activism-905600/ Accessed 31/1/2020.

15 Haidt, J. & Lukianoff, G. (2019). *The Coddling of the American Mind: How Good Intentions and Bad Ideas Are Setting Up a Generation for Failure*. London: Penguin.

16 Horowitz, A. (2013). *On Looking. Even Walks with Experts*. London: Scribner.

17 Horowitz (2013), p. 324.

18 Of course, schemata are psychologists' constructions to make sense of how we make sense of the world.

19 Wood (2018), p. 30.

20 Katz, D. (1960). The Functional Approach to the Study of Attitudes. *Public Opinion Quarterly*, 24, pp. 163–204.

21 Bartlett, F.C. (1932). *Remembering: A Study in Experimental and Social Psychology*. Cambridge University Press. See: www.bartlett.psychol.cam.ac.uk/Conventional isation.htm. Accesses 27/2/2020.

22 McCleod, S. (2018). Eyewitness Testimony. *Simply Psychology*. See: www.sim plypsychology.org/eyewitness-testimony.html. Accessed 1/3/2020.

23 Sharf, Z. (2018). 'Bohemian Rhapsody' Called Out for Factual Inaccuracies, Including 'Cruel' Handling of Freddie Mercury's HIV Diagnosis. *Indie Wire*. See: www.indiewire.com/2018/11/bohemian-rhapsody-called-out-chang ing-history-freddie-mercury-aids-1202018135/. Accessed 16/4/2020.

24 Tupper, E.F. (1973). *The Theology of Wolfhart Pannenberg*. Philadelphia: Westminster Press, pp. 100, 221.

25 Purser, R.E. & Millio, J. (2015). Mindfulness Revisited: A Buddhist-Based Conceptualization. *Journal of Management Inquiry*, 24 (1), pp. 3–24. Scherer, B. & Waistell, J. (2018). Incorporating Mindfulness: Questioning Capitalism. *Journal of Management, Spirituality & Religion*, 15 (2), pp. 123–140.

26 Purser, R. (2019) *McMindfulness: How Mindfulness Became the New Capitalist Spirituality*. London: Repeater.

27 Referencing Karl Marx's appraisal of religion – 'opium of the people'.

28 Purser (2019). And, Brazier, D. (2001). Zen Therapy. A Buddhist Approach to Psychotherapy. London: Robinson. Parker, I. (2020). *Psychology Through Critical Auto-Ethnography*. Oxford: Routledge, p. 3.

29 Blanco-Suarez, E. (2017). The Neuroscience of Loneliness. *Psychology Today*. www.psychologytoday.com/us/blog/brain-chemistry/201712/the-neuro science-loneliness. Accessed 1/3/2020.

30 Wood, G. (2008). *Don't Wait for Your Ship to Come In, Swim Out to Meet It*. Chichester: Capstone.

31 Blanco-Suarez (2017). See also: Cacioppo, J.T. & Cacioppo, S. (2018). The Growing Problem of Loneliness. *The Lancet*, 391 (10119), p. 426.

32 Wood (2008).

33 Mao, F. (2020). Coronavirus Panic: Why Are People Stockpiling Toilet Paper? *BBC News*. See: www.bbc.co.uk/news/world-australia-51731422. Accessed 12/3/2020. Also: Mental Health Foundation (2020). Looking After Your

Mental Health During the Coronavirus Outbreak. See: www.mentalhealth. org.uk/publications/looking-after-your-mental-health-during-coronavi rus-outbreak. Accessed 12/3/2020.

34 Purser & Millio (2015).

35 Baumeister, R.F. (2011). Self and Identity: A Brief Overview of What They Are, What They Do, and How They Work. *Annals of the New York Academy of Sciences*, 1234 (1), pp. 48–55.

36 Baumeister (2011).

37 Dennett, D.C. (1992). The self as a Center of Narrative Gravity. In: F. Kessel, P. Cole & D. Johnson (eds.) *Self and Consciousness: Multiple Perspectives*. Hillsdale, NJ: Erlbaum. See: http://cogprints.org/266/1/selfctr.htm. Accessed 5/7/2019. And: Jussim, L. & Ashmore, R.D. (1997). *Self and Identity: Fundamental Issues*. Oxford: Oxford University Press.

38 Jussim & Ashmore (1997).

39 Wood, G. (2013). *Unlock Your Confidence*. London: Watkins.

40 Selfie: the arm's-length photographic self-portraits that started off in bathroom mirrors – before the advent of selfie-sticks (to extend our reach) and when mobile phones had only one camera.

41 Ward, B., Ward, M., Fried, O. & Paskhover, B. (2018). Nasal Distortion in Short-Distance Photographs: The Selfie Effect. *JAMA Facial Plastic Surgery*, 20 (4), pp. 333–335. See: https://jamanetwork.com/journals/jamafacialplas ticsurgery/fullarticle/2673450. Accessed 3/3/2020.

42 Kelly, H. (2013). 7 Tips for Taking Better Selfies. *CNN Business*. See: https:// edition.cnn.com/2013/12/11/tech/mobile/selfie-photo-tips/. Accessed 3/3/2020.

43 And if you wish to marvel at your results, take the test: Summers, G. (2018). Can We Guess Who You Are in Only 20 Questions? *Playbuzz*. www.playbuzz.com/ gregs/can-we-guess-who-you-are-in-only-20-questions. Accessed 24/1/2020.

44 Manford, H., Kuhn, M.H. & McPartland, T.S. (1954). An Empirical Investigation of self-Attitudes. *American Sociological Review*, 19 (1), pp. 68–76. See: http://stelar.edc.org/sites/stelar.edc.org/files/Kuhn_TwentyStatementsT est.pdf. Accessed 28/1/2020.

45 Office for National Statistics (2018). Personal Well-Being User Guide. See: www.ons.gov.uk/peoplepopulationandcommunity/wellbeing/methodolo gies/personalwellbeingsurveyuserguide. Accessed 28/2/2020.

46 Office of National Statistics – ONS (2020). Personal and Economic Well-Being in the UK: February 2020. See: www.ons.gov.uk/peoplepopulationandcommunity/ wellbeing/bulletins/personalandeconomicwellbeingintheuk/february2020. Accessed 28/2/2020.

47 For the definition of ikigai see: www.definitions.net/definition/ikigai. Accessed 20/4/2020.

48 Misselbrook, D. (2014). W Is for Wellbeing and the WHO Definition of Health. *British Journal of General Practice*, 64 (628), p. 582. See: www.ncbi.nlm. nih.gov/pmc/articles/PMC4220217/. Accessed 21/4/2020.

49 See: Universal Declaration of Human Rights. United Nations. See: www.un.org/ en/universal-declaration-human-rights/index.html. Accessed 20/4/2020.

50 Bambra, C., Fox, D. & Scott-Samuel, A. (2005). Towards a Politics of Health. *Health Promotion International*, 20 (2), pp. 187–193. doi:10.1093/heapro/ dah608.

51 Harper, D. (2015). Psychologists Against Austerity. *The Psychologist*. https:// thepsychologist.bps.org.uk/volume-28/march-2015/psychologmai sts-against-austerity. Accessed 1/4/2020.

52 Mellor, M. (2019). Austerity Was Based on a Fairytale About Money. *The London Economic*. www.thelondoneconomic.com/opinion/austerity-was-based- on-a-fairytale-about-money/24/06/. Accessed 1/4/2020. Also: Broait, F. (2017). The Truth Behind the 'Magic Money Tree'. *Positive Money*. https://pos itivemoney.org/2017/06/magic-money-tree/. Accessed 1/4/2020.

53 Therrien, A. (2018). Life Expectancy Progress in UK 'Stops for First Time'. *BBC News*. www.bbc.co.uk/news/health-45638646. Accessed 18/4/2020.

54 GDP – gross domestic product – measures the total value of all of the goods made and services provided during a specific period of time. See: www.gov. uk/government/news/gross-domestic-product-gdp-what-it-means-and- why-it-matters. Accessed 21/4/2020.

55 Kinderman, P. (2015). Why Are Governments Interested in Our Wellbe- ing? *World Economic Forum*. See: www.weforum.org/agenda/2015/09/why- are-governments-interested-in-our-wellbeing/. Accessed 1/4/2020. See also: Stratton, A. (2010). Happiness Index to Gauge Britain's National Mood. *The Guardian*. See: www.theguardian.com/lifeandstyle/2010/nov/14/happi ness-index-britain-national-mood. Accessed 20/4/2020.

56 BBC News (2010). Plan to Measure Happiness 'Not Woolly' – Cameron. See: www.bbc.co.uk/news/uk-11833241. Accessed 21/4/2020.

57 Wilkinson, R. & Pickett, K. (2009). *The Spirit Level: Why More Equal Societies Almost Always Do Better*. London: Allen Lane.

58 Rowlingson, K. (2011). *Does Income Inequality Cause Health and Social Problems?* Joseph Rowntree Foundation. www.jrf.org.uk/report/does-income-inequal ity-cause-health-and-social-problems. Accessed 20/4/2020.

59 Fisher, P. & Alita Nandi, A. (2015). Poverty Across Ethnic Groups Through Reces- sion and Austerity. *Joseph Rowntree Foundation*. See: www.jrf.org.uk/report/pover ty-across-ethnic-groups-through-recession-and-austerity. Accessed 21/4/2020.

60 Milne, C. (2019). We Can't Explicitly Link 130,000 Preventable Deaths to Austerity. *Fullfact.org*. https://fullfact.org/health/130000-preventable-deaths-aus terity/. Accessed 18/4/2020. Also: Sippitt, A. (2017). Is Austerity Linked to 120,000 Unnecessary Deaths? *Fullfact.org*. See: https://fullfact.org/health/ austerity-120000-unnecessary-deaths/. Accessed 18/4/2020. Also: Helm, T. (2019). Austerity to Blame for 130,000 'Preventable' UK Deaths – Report. *The Guardian*. www.theguardian.com/politics/2019/jun/01/perfect-storm-aus terity-behind-130000-deaths-uk-ippr-report. Accessed 18/4/2020.

61 Therrien, A. (2018). Life Expectancy Progress in UK 'Stops for First Time'. *BBC News*. www.bbc.co.uk/news/health-45638646. Accessed 18/4/2020.

62 *BBC News* (2019). Poverty in the UK is 'Systematic' and 'Tragic', Says UN Special Rapporteur. See: www.bbc.co.uk/news/uk-48354692. Accessed 20/4/2020. For full report see: United Nations General Assembly (2018). Report of the Special Rapporteur on Extreme Poverty and Human Rights on His Mission to the United States of America. See: https://undocs.org/A/ HRC/38/33/ADD.1. Accessed 20/4/2020.

63 Chernomas, R. & Hudson, I. (2009). Social Murder: The Long-Term Effects of Conservative Economic Policy. *International Journal of Health Services*, 39 (1), pp. 107– 121. See: www.ncbi.nlm.nih.gov/pubmed/19326781. Accessed 21/4/2020.

64 Chu, B. (2015). The Wealth That Failed to Trickle Down: The Rich Do Get Richer While Poor Stay Poor, Report Suggests. *The Independent*. See: www. independent.co.uk/news/business/analysis-and-features/the-wealth-that-failed-to-trickle-down-report-suggests-rich-do-get-richer-while-poor-stay-poor-9989183.html. Accessed 30/4/2020. Fisher, M. & Bubola, E. (2020). As Coronavirus Deepens Inequality, Inequality Worsens Its Spread. *New York Times*. www.nytimes.com/2020/03/15/world/europe/coronavirus-ine quality.html. Accessed 17/4/2020. Also: Toynbee, P. (2020). Coronavirus Will Brutally Expose the Effect of a Decade of Public Service Cuts. *The Guardian*. See: www.theguardian.com/commentisfree/2020/mar/05/coronavi rus-epidemic-decade-austerity-public-services. Accessed 17/4/2020.

65 Atkinson, A. (2020). George Osborne, Architect of U.K. Austerity, Says New Cuts Needed Post-Crisis. *Bloomberg*. See: www.bloomberg.com/news/arti cles/2020-04-20/architect-of-u-k-austerity-says-retrenchment-needed-post-crisis. Accessed 21/4/2020.

66 Bulman, M. (2019). Austerity Measures and Hostile Environment 'Entrench ing Racism' in UK, Says UN. *The Independent*. www.independent.co.uk/news/ uk/home-news/austerity-racism-hostile-environment-xenophobia-un-re port-rapporteur-immigration-bame-a8959866.html. Accessed 15/2/2020.

67 Evans, A. (2020). Emily Maitlis Warns Coronavirus Is Not a 'Great Leveller' as the Lower Paid Suffer More in Powerful BBC Newsnight Speech. *iNews*. https://

inews.co.uk/news/health/emily-maitlist-bbc-newsnight-speech-coronavi
rus-warning-video-2534214. Accessed 18/4/2020.

68 Booth, R. (2020). BAME Groups Hit Harder by Covid-19 Than White People, UK Study Suggest. *The Guardian*. www.theguardian.com/world/2020/
apr/07/bame-groups-hit-harder-covid-19-than-white-people-uk. Accessed
1/5/2020. And: *BBC News* (2020). Coronavirus Wreaks Havoc in African
American Neighbourhoods. See: www.bbc.co.uk/news/world-us-canada-
52194018. Accessed 1/5/2020.

69 Siddique, H. (2020).UK Government Urged to Investigate Coronavirus Deaths of BAME Doctors. *The Guardian*. www.theguardian.com/soci
ety/2020/apr/10/uk-coronavirus-deaths-bame-doctors-bma. Accessed
17/4/2020.

70 Dixon, H. (2020). PPE: Government Counted Each Glove as Single Item to
Reach One Billion Total, Investigation Shows. *The Telegraph*. www.telegraph.
co.uk/politics/2020/04/28/ppe-government-counted-glove-single-item-
reach-one-billion-total/. Accessed 1/5/2020.

71 Adams, G. (2020). How WAS Flagship BBC Show Infiltrated by the Left?
When Panorama Turned Its Guns on the PPE Crisis, Five Medics Savaged
the Tories' Approach. Yet They ALL Had Labour Links, Writes GUY ADAMS.
The Daily Mail. www.dailymail.co.uk/news/article-8270999/How-Panora
ma-infiltrated-Left-BBC-interviewed-five-medics-Labour-links-PPE.html.
Accessed 1/5/2020.

72 Funke, M., Moritz Schularick, M. & Trebesch, C. (2016). Going to
Extremes: Politics After Financial Crises, 1870–2014. *European Economic
Review*, 88, pp. 227–260. See: www.sciencedirect.com/science/article/pii/
S0014292116300587. Accessed 1/5/2020.

73 Rampell, C. (2016). The Dangerous New Age of Global Autarky. *The Washington
Post*. www.washingtonpost.com/opinions/the-dangerous-new-age-of-autar
ky/2016/06/06/7338791e-2c21-11e6-b5db-e9bc84a2c8e4_story.html.
Accessed 1/5/2020.

74 Bulman (2019).

75 Walker, S. (2020). Hungary Passes Law That Will Let Orbán Rule by
Decree. *The Guardian*. www.theguardian.com/world/2020/mar/30/hunga
ry-jail-for-coronavirus-misinformation-viktor-orban. Accessed 1/5/2020.

76 *Pleasantville* (1998), directed by Gary Ross.

77 Definition of 'woke' from Merriam-Webster Dictionary. See: www.merri
am-webster.com/dictionary/woke. Accessed 3/5/2020.

78 Foley, M. (2016). What Does 'Woke' Mean? There's More to the Slang Term Than You Think. www.bustle.com/articles/134893-what-does-woke-mean-theres-more-to-the-slang-term-than-you-think. Accessed 4/5/2020.

79 Myers, L. (2019). Why Being 'Woke' Without Doing the Work Is Detrimental. *Milwaukee Courier*. See: https://milwaukeecourieronline.com/index.php/2019/12/06/why-being-woke-without-doing-the-work-is-detrimental/. Accessed 4/5/2020.

80 Barr, S. (2019). Barack Obama Calls Out Cancel Culture: 'That's Not Activism, That's Not Bringing About Change'. *The Independent*. See: www.independent.co.uk/life-style/barack-obama-cancel-culture-woke-activism-social-media-interview-yara-shahidi-a9177396.html. Accessed 4/5/2020.

81 Rose, S. (2020). How the Word 'Woke' Was Weaponised by the Right. *The Guardian*. www.theguardian.com/society/shortcuts/2020/jan/21/how-the-word-woke-was-weaponised-by-the-right. Accessed 4/5/2020.

82 Muder, D. (2012). The Distress of the Privileged. *Blog:The Weekly Sift*. https://weeklysift.com/2012/09/10/the-distress-of-the-privileged/. Accessed 3/5/2020.

83 Cited in Wood (2018), p. 63, as the website source link is broken for the interview with the director. *Pleasantville* (1998), directed by Gary Ross.

84 Quote Investigator could not definitively attribute this quote to a single source. See: https://quoteinvestigator.com/2016/10/24/privilege/. Accessed 18/4/2020.

85 Edelman Trust Barometer. See: www.edelman.com/trustbarometer. Accessed 4/5/2020.

86 Toynbee, P. (2020). Coronavirus Will Brutally Expose the Effect of a Decade of Public Service Cuts. *The Guardian*. www.theguardian.com/commentisfree/2020/mar/05/coronavirus-epidemic-decade-austerity-public-services. Accessed 6/3/2020.

87 Busby, M. (2020). 'The Government Has Abandoned Us': Gig Economy Workers Struggle to Cope. *The Guardian*. www.theguardian.com/business/2020/mar/17/the-government-has-abandoned-us-gig-economy-workers-struggle-to-cope. Accessed 17/4/2020.

88 Poem: *No Man Is an Island*, by John Donne. See: https://allpoetry.com/No-man-is-an-island. Accessed 29/3/2020.

89 Evans, A. (2020). Jeremy Corbyn Says Covid-19 Shows 'No One Is an Island' in Final PMQs as Labour Leader. *iNews*. See: https://inews.co.uk/news/pmqs-jeremy-corbyn-covid-19-labour-leader-coronavirus-2518245. Accessed 29/3/2020.

90 Steinmetz, K. (2020). She Coined the Term 'Intersectionality' Over 30 Years Ago. Here's What It Means to Her Today. *Time*. See: https://time.com/5786710/kimberle-crenshaw-intersectionality/. Accessed 6/3/2020.

91 IWDA (2018).What Does Intersectional Feminism Actually Mean? *International Women's Development Agency*. About us. See: https://iwda.org.au/what-does-intersectional-feminism-actually-mean/. Accessed 19/4/2020.

92 Crenshaw quoted in Steinmetz (2020).

93 Borstein, K. (1998). *My Gender Workbook*. London & New York: Routledge. Kate identifies as non-binary and her website uses female pronouns. http://katebornstein.com/. Accessed 19/4/2020.

94 Crenshaw quoted in Steinmetz (2020).

95 Brannon (2017) cited in Wood (2018), pp. 54–55.

96 Crenshaw quoted in Steinmetz (2020).

CHAPTER 4

1 Wheeler Johnson, M. (2013). Burnout Is Everywhere – Here's What Countries Are Doing to Fix It. *Huff Post*. See: www.huffingtonpost.co.uk/entry/worker-burnout-worldwide-governments_n_3678460?ri18n=true. Accessed 1/4/2020.

2 Work-related stress, anxiety or depression statistics in Great Britain (2019). Health and Safety Executive. See: www.hse.gov.uk/statistics/causdis/stress.pdf. Accessed 19/4/2020.

3 Mohney, G. (2018). Stress Costs U.S. $300 Billion Every Year. *Healthline*. See: www.healthline.com/health-news/stress-health-costs#1. Accessed 19/4/2020. And: Brondolo, E., Byer, K., Gianaros, P.J., Liu, C., Prather, A.A., Thomas, K. & Woods-Giscombé, C.L. (2017). Stress and Heath Disparities. Contexts, Mechanisms, and Interventions Among Racial/Ethnic Minority and Low Socioeconomic Status Populations. American Psychological Association. www.apa.org/pi/health-disparities/resources/stress-report.pdf. Accessed 25/4/2020.

4 Misselbrook, D. (2014). W Is for Wellbeing and the WHO Definition of Health. *British Journal of General Practice*, 64 (628), p. 582. See: www.ncbi.nlm.nih.gov/pmc/articles/PMC4220217/. Accessed 21/4/2020.

5 Poem: 'The Unknown Citizen' by W.H. Auden (1907–1973). Poets.org: See: https://poets.org/poem/unknown-citizen. Accessed 17/4/2020. I had hoped to reproduce the poem but did not receive a reply in time for permission to use it.

6 Lindner, R. (1952, 1971). *The Revolutionist's Handbook*. New York: Grove Press, p. 67.

7 Sketch from Episode 32. The show ran from 1969 to 1974 on BBC TV.

8 Sims, A. (2015). The European Countries That Wash Their Hands Least After Going to the Toilet. *The Independent*. See: www.independent.co.uk/news/world/europe/the-european-countries-that-wash-their-hands-least-after-going-to-the-toilet-a6757711.html. Accessed 25/4/2020. See also: Timins, H. (2020). Hands Down, Men Worse at Bathroom Hygiene That Prevents Coronavirus. *Reuters*. www.reuters.com/article/us-health-coronavirus-hand washing-idUSKBN20S2N7. Accessed 25/4/2020.

9 For example, Gross, R.D. (2015). *Psychology; The Science of Mind and Behaviour* (7th ed.). London: Hodder Education.

10 Jahoda, M. (1958). Joint Commission on Mental Health and Illness Monograph Series: Vol. 1. Current Concepts of Positive Mental Health. *Basic Books*. https://doi.org/10.1037/11258-000.

11 Jahoda, M. (2009). *Employment and Unemployment: A Social-Psychological Analysis* (The Psychology of Social Issues). Cambridge: Cambridge University Press.

12 Maslow, A.H. (1987). *Motivation and Personality* (3rd ed.). London: Pearson Education.

13 Lindner, R. (1952, 1971). *The Revolutionist's Handbook*. New York: Grove Press, p. 4.

14 My paraphrase (not a direct quotation) from Dodge, R., Daly, A., Huyton, J. & Sanders, L. (2012). The Challenge of Defining Wellbeing. *International Journal of Wellbeing*, 2 (3), 222–235. doi:10.5502/ijw.v2i3.4. Accessed 3/5/2020.

15 Cox, T. (1975). The Nature and Management of Stress. *New Behaviour*, 25, pp. 493–495.

16 McCleod, S. (2010). Stress and Live Events. *Simply Psychology*. www.simplypsychology.org/SRRS.html. Accessed 28/4/2020. Take the Holmes and Rahe Stress Test at: www.mindtools.com/pages/article/newTCS_82.htm. Accessed 28/4/2020. Taking the test in the final week of writing this book, in lockdown, I scored 327!

17 Rahe, R.H. & Arthur, R.J. (1978). Life Change and Illness Studies: Past History and Future Directions. *Journal of Human Stress*, 4 (1), pp. 3–15.

18 Canadian Medical Hall of Fame (no date). Hans Selye, MD PhD. See: www.cdnmedhall.org/inductees/hansselye. Accessed 28/4/2020.

19 The term 'fight or flight' was coined by physiologist Walter Cannon in 1915.

20 American Psychological Association. (no date). See: www.apa.org/help center/stress-body. Accessed 5/5/2020.

21 Wood, G.W. (2019). *Letters to a New Student. Tips to Study Smarter from a Psychologist.* London & New York: Routledge.

22 Given the Greek origins of each prefix, the two types of stress can be thought of as dystopian and utopian – loosely.

23 Yerkes, R.M. & Dodson, J.D. (1908). The Relation of Strength of Stimulus to Rapidity of Habit-formation. *Journal of Comparative Neurology and Psychology,* 18 (5), pp. 459–482.

24 Lazarus, R.S. & Folkman, S. (1984). *Stress, Appraisal and Coping.* New York: Springer, p. 19.

25 McLeod, S. (2015). Stress Management. *Simply Psychology.* See: www.simplyp sychology.org/stress-management.html. Accessed 3/5/2020. And: Penley, J.A., Tomaka, J. & Wiebe, J.S. (2002). The Association of Coping to Physical and Psychological Health Outcomes: A Meta-analytic Review. *Journal of Behavioral Medicine,* 25 (6), pp. 551–603.

26 McLeod (2015). And: Penley et al. (2002).

27 Heid, M. (2018). You Asked: Is It Bad for You to Read the News Constantly? *Time.* See: https://time.com/5125894/is-reading-news-bad-for-you/ Accessed 9/5/2020.

28 Including Richard Lazarus.

29 Kanner, A.D., Coyne, J.C., Schaefer, C. & Lazarus, R.S. (1981). Comparison of Two Modes of Stress Measurement: Daily Hassles and Uplifts Versus Major Life Events. *Journal of Behavioral Medicine,* 4 (1), pp. 1–39.

30 Maddi, S. (2002). The Story of Hardiness: Twenty Years of Theorizing, Research & Practice. *Consulting Psychology Journal: Practice and Research,* 54 (3), pp. 173–185.

31 Wood, G.W. (2019). *Letters to a New Student. Tips to Study Smarter from a Psychologist.* London & New York: Routledge. The book is based on a series of brief, problem-page style letters that can be read in any order. It is based on three factors: *foundation, managing obstacles,* and *practical psychology.*

32 Katz, D. (1960) cited in Wood (2019). And: Berg, I.K. & Szabo, P. (2005). *Brief Coaching for Lasting Solutions.* London: W.W. Norton.

33 Selhub (2005), Pinilla (2008) and Lieberman (2013), all cited in Wood (2019).

34 Rhodes (2013) cited in Wood (2019).

35 Quan (2016), Alhola & Polo-Kantola (2007), and Gordon (2013), all cited in Wood (2019).

36 Jones & Gould (1996) cited in Wood (2019).

37 Watson (2015) and Lange (2013), both cited in Wood (2019).

38 Bryom (2016), Webb (2016), Lazarus & Folkman (1984), also cited in Wood (2019).

39 Kabat-Zinn (1994) cited in Bazin, O. & Kuyken, W. (2017). The Mindfulness Approach. Promises and Perils in the 21st Century. *Psychology Review*, November, pp. 20–23.

40 Wolpe (1991) cited in Wood (2019).

41 Hardy et al. (1996) cited in Wood (2019).

42 Bazin & Kuyken (2017), pp. 20–23.

43 Briers, S. (2012). *Psychobabble. Exploding the Myths of the self-Help Generation*. London: Pearson, p. 73.

44 Briers (2012).

45 Briers (2012), p. 73.

46 Luborsky et al. (1975) cited in Bergsma (2007). But originally: S. Rosenzweig (1936). Some Implicit Common Factors in Diverse Methods of Psychotherapy. *American Journal of Orthopsychiatry*, 6 (3), pp. 412–415. https://doi.org/10.1111/j.1939-0025.1936.tb05248.x.

47 Briers (2012).

48 Hubble & Miller (2004) cited in Bergsma (2007).

49 Talmon, M. (1990). *Single Session Therapy: Maximizing the Effect of the First (and Often Only) Therapeutic Encounter*. Chichester: Jossey-Bass.

50 See: https://twitter.com/matthaig1/status/1256982826978873344. Accessed 7/5/2020.

51 *BBC News* (2020). Coronavirus: Book Sales Surge as Readers Seek Escapism and Education. www.bbc.co.uk/news/entertainment-arts-52048582. Accessed 7/5/2020. Also: *The Telegraph* (2020). Reading 'Can Help Reduce Stress'. www.telegraph.co.uk/news/health/news/5070874/Reading-can-help-reduce-stress.html. Accessed 7/5/2020.

52 Family Links (no date). Emotional Health and Wellbeing – Good Mental Health Starts Here. See: www.familylinks.org.uk/post/emotional-health-and-wellbeing-good-mental-health-starts-here. Accessed 7/5/2020.

CHAPTER 5

1 Salermo, S. (2005). *SHAM. How the Gurus of the self-help Movement Makes Us Helpless*. London & Boston: Nicholas Brealey.

2 An infomercial is a form of television commercial, which generally includes a free telephone number or website.

3 LaRosa, J. (2018). The $10 Billion self-Improvement Market Adjusts to a New Generation. *MarketReasrch.com blog*. See: https://blog.marketresearch.com/the-10-billion-self-improvement-market-adjusts-to-new-generation. Accessed 22/4/2020.

4 Metcalf, T. (no date). The self Improvement Industry. *Bizfluent*. See: https://bizfluent.com/13355649/the-self-improvement-industry. Accessed 22/4/2020.

5 Flood, A. (2017). Sales of Mind, Body, Spirit Books Boom in UK Amid 'Mindfulness Mega-trend'. *The Guardian*. See: www.theguardian.com/books/2017/jul/31/sales-of-mind-body-spirit-books-boom-in-uk-amid-mindfulness-mega-trend. Accessed 22/4/2020.

6 Flood, A. (2020). Mrs Hinch Cleans Up with Book Sales as Britons Tidy Homes in Lockdown. *The Guardian*. www.theguardian.com/books/2020/apr/08/mrs-hinch-cleans-up-with-book-sales-as-britons-tidy-homes-in-lockdown. Accessed 22/4/2020.

7 I confess that I've written a few self-help books, and you can be the judge of which category mine fall into.

8 And I cleaned that one up for a family audience. Iron pyrite is nicknamed 'fool's gold' due to its resemblance to gold, but it sometimes has tiny flecks of the real stuff.

9 The inscription above the gates of hell in 'Inferno', the first part of Dante Alighieri's (1265–1321) epic poem *Divine Comedy*.

10 The original title for this chapter was 'Is self-help bad for your health and wellbeing?' However, feedback at the proposal stage for the book questioned whether such a title might alienate self-help readers. One of the aims of the book is to bridge the gap between pop psychology and academia.

11 As well as on radio and TV.

12 This is where the critical questions on 'unworthy authorities' in Chapter 2 are useful.

13 Papachristos, A. (2018). Reading For 6 Minutes Each Day Can Reduce Stress By 68 Percent, Study Says. *A Plus*. https://articles.aplus.com/a/reading-6-minutes-each-day-reduce-stress-68-percent. Accessed 5/5/2020.

14 Lehr, F. (1981). Bibliotherapy. *Journal of Reading*, 25 (1), pp. 76–79.

15 Pardeck, John T. (1993). *Using Bibliotherapy in Clinical Practice: A Guide to self-help Books* (Contributions in Psychology). CT: Greenwood Press.

16 See Merriam-Webster definition of self-help: www.merriam-webster.com/dictionary/self-help. Accessed 23/4/2020.

17 Pardeck (1993). And: Starker, S. (1989, 2002). *Oracle at the Supermarket; The American Preoccupation with self-help Books*. New Brunswick: Transaction Publishers.

18 Starker (1989, 2002).

19 Bergsma, A. (2008). Do self-help Books Help? *Journal of Happiness Studies*, 9, pp. 341–360. See: https://doi.org/10.1007/s10902-006-9041-2. Accessed 23/4/2020.

20 The book in question was Wood, G. (2008). *Don't Wait for Your Ship to Come In . . . Swim Out to Meet It!* Chichester: Capstone. Sadly, the review on Amazon has now been removed.

21 Salerno (2005). Wood, G. (2013). *Unlock Your Confidence*. London: Warkins.

22 Starker (1989, 2002).

23 Bergsma (2008).

24 Wilson & Ash (2000) cited in Bergsma (2008).

25 Weekbladpers Tijdschriften (2004) cited in Bergsma (2008).

26 Veenhoven (1988) cited in Bergsma (2008).

27 Gaille, B. (2017). 19 self Improvement Industry Statistics and Trends.BrandonGaille.com See: https://brandongaille.com/18-self-improvement-industry-statistics-and-trends/. Accessed 24/4/2020.

28 de Botton, A. (2012). In Defence of self-help Books. *The Guardian*. See: www.theguardian.com/commentisfree/2012/may/17/in-defence-of-self-help-books. Accessed 22/2/2020.

29 Zhou, Y. (2017). Goodreads Data Show That Women Reading self-help Books Are Getting Advice from Men. *Quartz*. See: https://qz.com/1106341/most-women-reading-self-help-books-are-getting-advice-from-men/. Accessed 22/4/2020.

30 Wood, G.W. (2018). *The Psychology of Gender*. London & New York: Routledge.

31 Zhou (2017).

32 Cuijpers (1997) cited in Bergsma (2008). A meta-analysis is a statistical analysis that combines the results of multiple studies.

33 Willemse et al. (2004) cited in Bergsma (2008).

34 Bergsma (2008).

35 Mains & Scoggins (2003) cited in Bergsma (2008).

36 Bergsman (2008).

37 *Self-Help* was published during the third cholera pandemic of 1846–1860. Coincidentally, two of the most popular self-help titles were published in the 1930s during the Great Depression. These were *How to Win Friends and Influence People* (1932) by Dale Carnegie and *Think and Grow Rich* (1937) by Napoleon Hill. So whether we will see a slew of post-pandemic self-help titles – embracing solicitude, ecology, home cooking, and cleaning – remains to be seen.

38 Mark, K. (2009). Samuel Smiles and self-help. *The Encyclopedia of Pedagogy and Informal Education*. See: www.infed.org/thinkers/samuel_smiles_self_help.

htm. Accessed 22/4/2020. Also: British Library Collection Items (no date). self-Help by Samuel Smiles. See: www.bl.uk/collection-items/self-help-by-samuel-smiles. Accessed 22/4/2020.

39 Mark (2009). Also: British Library Collection Items (no date).

40 Liker, Jeffrey K. (2004). *The Toyota Way*. McGraw Hill, p. 17.

41 Appiah, K.A. (2018). The Myth of Meritocracy: Who Really Gets What They Deserve? *The Guardian*. www.theguardian.com/news/2018/oct/19/the-myth-of-meritocracy-who-really-gets-what-they-deserve. Accessed 29/4/2020.

42 Smiles, S. (1897). *self-Help with Illustrations of Conduct and Perseverance* (Popular ed.). London: John Murray. See: www.gutenberg.org/files/935/935-h/935-h.htm. Accessed 24/4/2020.

43 British Library Collection Items (no date).

44 New Economics Foundation (2013). *Framing the Economy: The Austerity Story*. London: New Economics Foundation.

45 Davis, L.J. (2009). *Obsession: A History*. Chicago: University of Chicago Press, p. 173.

46 That's why 'All You Need to Know to Change Your Life in Seven Days' usually has a follow-up, then another, and another, and another.

47 I'm quite pleased with that phrase.

48 These are composites, not actual quotations.

49 Briers, S. (2012). *Psychobabble. Exploding the Myths of the Self-Help Generation*. London: Pearson.

50 Attributed to Les Brown. Apologies to him.

51 Van Prooijen, J-W. (2018). *The Psychology of Conspiracy Theories*. London & New York: Routledge. Myers (2002) and Stanovich (2007) both cited in Lilienfeld et al. (2010), p. 4.

52 Hyde, J.S. (2005). Gender Similarities Hypothesis. *American Psychologist*, 60 (6), pp. 581–592. For a review of the research see my book: Wood (2018).

53 Rippon, G. (2015) cited in Wood (2018).

54 Sperry, R.W. (1968). Hemisphere Deconnection and Unity in Conscious Awareness. *American Psychologist*, 23 (10), 723.

55 Nielsen et al. (2013) cited in Wood (2018).

56 Lilienfeld, S.O. (2010). *50 Great Myths of Popular Psychology. Shattering Widespread Misconceptions About Human Behaviour*. Chichester: Wiley-Blackwell.

57 Thyer, B.A. & Pignotti, M.G. (2015). *Science and Pseudoscience in Social Work Practice*. New York: Springer Publishing Company. And: Witkowski, T. (2010). Thirty-Five Years of Research on Neuro-Linguistic Programming. NLP Research Data Base. State of the Art or Pseudoscientific Decoration?

Polish Psychological Bulletin, 41 (2). See: http://journals.pan.pl/dlibra/publi cation/114591/edition/99644/content. And: Sharpley, C.F. (1987). Research Findings on Neurolinguistic Programming: Nonsupportive Data or an Untestable Theory? *Journal of Counseling Psychology*, 34 (1), pp. 103–107. doi:10.1037/0022-0167.34.1.103.

58 BBC *News* (2009). Cat Registered as Hypnotherapist. http://news.bbc. co.uk/1/hi/8303126.stm. Accessed 29/4/2020.

59 Wood, G. (2009). Blogpost: Body Language Myth: The 7%–38%–55% Rule. https://psycentral.wordpress.com/2009/03/03/body-language-myth-7-38-55-rule-dr-gary-wood-psycholog/. Accessed 29/4/2020.

60 Harrison, T. (2020). The Horror of Toxic Positivity: Why Positive Thinking Can Be Harmful. *The Mind Journal*. See: https://themindsjournal.com/tox ic-positivity/. Accessed 5/5/2020.

61 Jahoda, M. (1958). Joint Commission on Mental Health and Illness Mono-graph Series: Vol. 1. *Current Concepts of Positive Mental Health*. Basic Books. https://doi.org/10.1037/11258-000.

62 Ehrenreich, B. (2010). *Smile or Die. How Positive Thinking Fooled America & the World*. London: Granta.

63 Salerno (2005).

64 Wood, G. (2010). Look Out! Look Out! Psychobabble Blue Monday Is About! The Most Gullible Day of the Year. https://psycentral.wordpress.com/2010/01/17/ psychobabble-blue-monday-psychology/. Accessed 2/5/2020.

65 McCaugherty, S. (2020). WATCH: Dr. Phil Responds to Criticism After Com-ments on Fox News. *Heavy*. https://heavy.com/news/2020/04/dr-phil-re sponds-criticism/. Accessed 2/5/2020. And: McCaugherty, S. (2020). Dr. Oz Under Fire After '2–3 Percent' Trade-Off for Opening Schools Com-ment. *Heavy*. https://heavy.com/news/2020/04/dr-oz-reopening-schools/. Accessed 2/5/2020.

66 Korownyk, C., Kolber, M.R., McCormack, J., Lam, V., Overbo, K., Candra Cotton, C., Finley, C., Turgeon, R.D., Garrison, S., Lindblad, A.J., Banh, H.L., Campbell-Scherer, D., Vandermeer, B. & Allan, G.M. (2014). Televised Medi-cal Talk Shows – What They Recommend and the Evidence to Support Their Recommendations: A Prospective Observational Study. *BMJ*, 349, g7346. doi: https://doi.org/10.1136/bmj.g7346. Accessed 20/6/2019.

67 Although Salerno tends to get a bit carried away and only stops short of blaming the self-help industry for the fall of Rome.

68 M.C. Escher (1898–1972) was a Dutch graphic artist who made mathemat-ically inspired woodcuts including impossible objects and explorations of infinity.

69   Bateson, G., Jackson, D.D., Haley, J. & Weakland, J. (1956). Toward a Theory of Schizophrenia. *Behavioral Science*, 1, pp. 251–264.

70   Laing, R.D. (1970). *Knots*. London: Penguin.

71   Moberly, N.J. & Dickson, J.M. (2018). Goal Conflict, Ambivalence and Psychological Distress: Concurrent and Longitudinal Relationships. *Personality and Individual Differences*, 129, pp. 38–42. doi:10.1016/j.paid.2018.03.008. Accessed 29/4/2020. www.researchgate.net/publication/323798202_Goal_conflict_ambivalence_and_psychological_distress_Concurrent_and_longitudinal_relationships.

72   Borstein, K. (1998). *My Gender Workbook*. London& New York: Routledge.

73   Pérez, J.E. (1999). Eysenck (1970) cited in Integration of Cognitive-Behavioral and Interpersonal Therapies for Latinos: An Argument for Technical Eclecticism. *Journal of Contemporary Psychotherapy*, 29 (3) pp. 169–183.

74   You could f**k off by yourself on a package deal and f**k it for a fraction of the f**king price.

75   Wood, G. (2013). 3 Tips to Get the Most from a self Help Book. https://psycentral.wordpress.com/2013/08/23/how-to-get-the-most-from-a-self-help-book-dr-gary-wood-life-coach-birmingham/. Accessed 24/4/2020.

76   Krauss Whitbourne, S. (2012). Five Things You Need to Know About self-Help Books. *Psychology Today*. See: www.psychologytoday.com/us/blog/fulfillment-any-age/201205/five-things-you-need-know-about-self-help-books. Accessed 24/4/2020.

77   See: Reading Well Website. https://reading-well.org.uk/.

78   Wood, G.W. (2019). *Letters to a New Student. Tips to Study Smarter from a Psychologist*. London & New York: Routledge.

79   Robinson (1970) cited in Wood (2019).

80   This depends on the nature of the issues you want to work on, so be aware of confidentiality issues.

81   P.S.: I once attended a one-day meditation workshop by a yogi named Clive, with a double-barrel surname, whose Tigger-like exuberance was only matched by the liveliness of his tie-dyed yoga pants. There is actually no point to this sentence, but I just wanted to share it with someone.

CHAPTER 6

1   Peterson, C. (2008). What Is Positive Psychology, and What Is It Not? *Psychology Today*. See: www.psychologytoday.com/us/blog/the-good-life/200805/what-is-positive-psychology-and-what-is-it-not. Accessed 26/4/2020.

2 Max, D.T. (2007). Happiness 101. *New York Times Magazine*. See: www.nytimes. com/2007/01/07/magazine/07happiness.t.html. Accessed 6/5/2020.

3 International Positive Psychology Association (no date). About IPPA. See: www.ippanetwork.org/about/. Accessed 6/5/2020.

4 McVeigh, T. (2011). David Cameron Measuring 'Wrong Type of Happiness'. *The Guardian*. See: www.theguardian.com/politics/2011/apr/10/david-cam eron-wrong-type-happiness. Accessed 6/5/2020.

5 Or else, they'd taken an instant dislike to me. Or they just didn't want to be there. Needless to say, I didn't accept the job offer. And over the next year the same post was advertised many times. I count it as a narrow escape.

6 Pronounced 'Mee-high Chick-sent-me-high', but Martin Seligman calls him 'Mike'.

7 Selihman, M. & Csikszenthihalyi, M. (2000). Positive Psychology: An Introduction. American Psychologist, 55(1), pp.5–14. See: DOI: 10.1037/0003-066X.55.1.5, p. 5.

8 Seligman & Csikszentmihalyi (2000), p. 13.

9 Seligman & Csikszentmihalyi (2000), p. 5.

10 Malow, A.H. (1997). Motivation and Personality, Third Edition. London: Pearson.

11 Froh, J.F. (2004). The History of Positive Psychology: Truth Be Told. NYS Psychologist, pp. 18–20.

12 Seligman, M. (2004). The New Era of Positive Psychology. *TED Talks*. See: www.ted.com/talks/martin_seligman_the_new_era_of_positive_psychol ogy. Accessed 27/4/2020.

13 Grenville-Cleave (2012). See also: Dodge, R., Daly, A., Huyton, J. & Sanders, L. (2012). The Challenge of Defining Wellbeing. *International Journal of Wellbeing*, 2 (3), pp. 222–235. doi:10.5502/ijw.v2i3.4.

14 The various scales on Ed Diener's website are free to use. See: https://eddi ener.com/scales. Accessed 27/4/2020.

15 Geirland, J. (1996). Go with the Flow. *Wired Magazine*, September, Issue 4.09. See: www.wired.com/1996/09/czik/. Accessed 2/5/2020.

16 Csikszentmihalyi, M. (1997). *Finding Flow:The Psychology of Engagement with Everyday Life*. New York: Perseus Books.

17 Wood, G.W. (2019). *Letters to a New Student.Tips to Study Smarter from a Psychologist*. London & New York: Routledge.

18 Geirland (1996).

19 McVeigh (2011).

20 Fredrickson, B.L. & Losada, M.F. (2005). Positive Affect and Complex Dynamics of Human Flourishing. *American Psychologist*, 60 (7), pp. 678–686. doi:10.1037/0003-066x.60.7.678.

21 Corey, L.M., Keyes, C.L.M. & Haidt, J. (2002). *Flourishing: Positive Psychology and the Life Well-Lived*. Washington: American Psychological Association.

22 Jahoda, M. (1958). Joint Commission on Mental Health and Illness Monograph Series: Vol. 1. *Current Concepts of Positive Mental Health*. Basic Books. https://doi.org/10.1037/11258-000. It's not surprising that Carol Ryff is the Marie Jahoda Professor of Psychology at the University of Wisconsin-Madison.

23 Video: How to Ikigai | Tim Tamashiro | TEDxYYC, See: https://youtu.be/pk-PcJS2QaU. Accessed 6/5/2020.

24 Mitsuhashi, Y. (2017). Ikigai: A Japanese Concept to Improve Work and Life. *BBC Worklife*. www.bbc.com/worklife/article/20170807-ikigai-a-japanese-concept-to-improve-work-and-life. Accessed 6/5/2020.

25 Kowalski, K. (2019). The Truth About Ikigai: Definitions, Diagrams & Myths About the Japanese Life Purpose. Sloww, see: www.sloww.co/ikigai/. Accessed 6//5/2020. See also: Kowalski, K. (2019). Ikigai 2.0: Evolving the Ikigai Diagram for Life Purpose (& Why and How It Needs to Be Redesigned). Sloww, see: www.sloww.co/ikigai-2-0/. Accessed 6/5/2020.

26 Kamiya (1966) cited in Nakanishi, N. (1999). Letter from Japan. 'Ikigai' in Older Japanese People. *Age and Ageing*, 28, pp. 323–324.

27 Nakanishi (1999).

28 Mitsuhashi (2017).

29 Yaden, D.B., Eichstaedt, J.C. & Medaglia, J.D. (2018). The Future of Technology in Positive Psychology: Methodological Advances in the Science of Well-Being. *Frontiers in Psychology*, 9, p. 962. doi:10.3389/fpsyg.2018.00962.

30 World Well-Being Project. About Us. See: www.wwbp.org/about.html. Accessed 10/5/2020.

31 Ehrenreich, B. (2009). *Smile or Die. How Positive Thinking Fooled America & the World*. London: Granta. See also: Andrew, A. (2014). The British Amateur Who Debunked the Mathematics of Happiness. *The Guardian*. See: www.theguardian.com/science/2014/jan/19/mathematics-of-happiness-debunked-nick-brown. Accessed 6/5/2020.

32 Joseph, J. (2013). The Trouble with Twin Studies. *Mad in America*. See: www.madinamerica.com/2013/03/the-trouble-with-twin-studies/. Accessed 27/4/2020.

33 Becker, D. & Marecek, J. (2008). Positive Psychology: History in the Remaking? *Theory in Psychology*, 18 (5), pp. 591–604. https://doi.org/10.1177/0959354308093397.

34 Huxley, A. (1932). *Brave New World*. London: Chatto & Windus.

35 Andreski, S. (1972). *Social Science as Sorcery*. London: Andre Deutsch. Quote taken from the dust jacket.

36 Schneider, K.J. (2010). Toward a Humanistic Positive Psychology: Why Can't We Just Get Along? *Psychology Today*. www.psychologytoday.com/ca/blog/awakening-awe/201011/toward-humanistic-positive-psychology-why-cant-we-just-get-along. Accessed 6/5/2020.

37 Gross, R. (2015). *Psychology. The Science of Mind and Behaviour*. London: Hodder Education.

38 Becker & Marecek (2008).

39 Quoted in Wood, G.W. (2018). *The Psychology of Gender*. London & New York: Routledge.

40 Greer (1999) cited in Wood (2019), p.81

CHAPTER 7

1 And despite the protestations of 'never again', the seeds of the next book began to form as I wrote this conclusion.

2 It was part of The Tanner Lectures on Human Values. It was given at the University of Michigan.

3 The racist connotations put on Nietzsche's work are attributed to the editing of his sister. See: Gray, J. (2016). Anti-Education by Friedrich Nietzsche Review – Why Mainstream Culture, Not the Universities, Is Doing Our Best Thinking. *The Guardian*. See: www.theguardian.com/books/2016/jan/08/anti-education-on-the-future-of-our-educational-institutions-friedrich-nietzsche-review. Accessed 10/5/2020.

4 Rocheleau, G. (2016). 3 Metamorphoses: Nietzsche's Map of Human Growth. See: www.updevelopment.org/3-metamorphoses-nietzsches-map-human-growth/ Accessed 10/5/2020.

5 Toffler, A. (1970). *Future Shock*. London: Pan Books.

6 A composite anecdote that seems to have begun with a version in 1951. Kelley, E.C. (1951). *The Workshop Way of Learning*. New York: Harper & Brothers, p. 2. It has been added to over the years. See: https://quoteinvestigator.com/2010/07/11/confused/. Accessed 26/4/2020.